Timelapse™

The Official Strategy Guide

Prima Publishing
Rocklin, California
(916) 632-4400

NOW AVAILABLE FROM PRIMA

Computer Game Books
1942: The Pacific Air War—The Official Strategy Guide
The 11th Hour: The Official Strategy Guide
The 7th Guest: The Official Strategy Guide
Aces Over Europe: The Official Strategy Guide
Across the Rhine: The Official Strategy Guide
Alone in the Dark 3: The Official Strategy Guide
Angel Devoid: The Official Strategy Guide
Armored Fist: The Official Strategy Guide
Ascendancy: The Official Strategy Guide
CD-ROM Games Secrets, Volume 1
CD-ROM Unauthorized Games Secrets, Volume 2
Caesar II: The Official Strategy Guide
Celtic Tales: Balor of the Evil Eye—The Official
    Strategy Guide
Cyberia: The Official Strategy Guide
Computer Adventure Games Secrets
Dark Seed II: The Official Strategy Guide
Descent: The Official Strategy Guide
DOOM Battlebook
DOOM II: The Official Strategy Guide
Dragon Lore: The Official Strategy Guide
Dungeon Master II: The Legend of Skullkeep—The
    Official Strategy Guide
Fleet Defender: The Official Strategy Guide
Frankenstein: Through the Eyes of the Monster—
    The Official Strategy Guide
Front Page Sports Football Pro '95: The Official
    Playbook
Fury3: The Official Strategy Guide
Hell: A Cyberpunk Thriller—The Official
    Strategy Guide
Heretic: The Official Strategy Guide
I Have No Mouth and I Must Scream: The Official
    Strategy Guide
In The 1st Degree: The Official Strategy Guide
Buried in Time: The Journeyman Project 2—The
    Official Strategy Guide
Kingdom: The Far Reaches—The Official Strategy
    Guide
King's Quest VII: The Unauthorized Strategy Guide
The Legend of Kyrandia: The Official Strategy Guide
Lords of Midnight: The Official Strategy Guide
Machiavelli the Prince: Official Secrets & Solutions
Marathon: The Official Strategy Guide
Master of Orion: The Official Strategy Guide
Master of Magic: The Official Strategy Guide
Mech Warrior 2: The Official Strategy Guide
Microsoft Arcade: The Official Strategy Guide
Microsoft Flight Simulator 5.1: The Official Strategy
    Guide
Microsoft Golf: The Official Strategy Guide
Microsoft Space Simulator: The Official Strategy Guide
Might and Magic Compendium: The Authorized
    Strategy Guide for Games I, II, III, and IV

Mission Critical: The Official Strategy Guide
Myst: The Official Strategy Guide, Revised Edition
Online Games: In-Depth Strategies and Secrets
Oregon Trail II: The Official Strategy Guide
The Pagemaster: Official CD-ROM Strategy Guide
Panzer General: The Official Strategy Guide
Perfect General II: The Official Strategy Guide
Power Pete: Official Secrets and Solutions
Prince of Persia: The Official Strategy Guide
Prisoner of Ice: The Official Strategy Guide
Rebel Assault: The Official Insider's Guide
The Residents: Bad Day on the Midway—The Official
    Strategy Guide
Return to Zork Adventurer's Guide
Romance of the Three Kingdoms IV: Wall of Fire—The
    Official Strategy Guide
Shadow of the Comet: The Official Strategy Guide
Shannara: The Official Strategy Guide
Sid Meier's Civilization, or Rome on 640K a Day
Sid Meier's Colonization: The Official Strategy Guide
SimCity 2000: Power, Politics, and Planning
SimEarth: The Official Strategy Guide
SimFarm Almanac: The Official Guide to SimFarm
SimIsle: The Official Strategy Guide
SimLife: The Official Strategy Guide
SimTower: The Official Strategy Guide
Stonekeep: The Official Strategy Guide
SubWar 2050: The Official Strategy Guide
Terry Pratchett's Discworld: The Official Strategy Guide
Thunderscape: The Official Strategy Guide
TIE Fighter: The Official Strategy Guide
TIE Fighter: Defender of the Empire—Official Secrets &
    Solutions
Ultima: The Avatar Adventures
Ultima VII and Underworld: More Avatar Adventures
Under a Killing Moon: The Official Strategy Guide
WarCraft: Orcs & Humans Official Secrets & Solutions
Warlords II Deluxe: The Official Strategy Guide
Werewolf Vs. Commanche: The Official Strategy Guide
Wing Commander I, II, and III: The Ultimate
    Strategy Guide
X-COM Terror From The Deep: The Official
    Strategy Guide
X-COM UFO Defense: The Official Strategy Guide
X-Wing: Collector's CD-ROM—The Official
Strategy Guide

How to Order:
For information on quantity discounts contact the publisher: Prima Publishing, P.O. Box 1260BK, Rocklin, CA
95677-1260; (916) 632-4400. On your letterhead
include information concerning the intended use of the
books and the number of books you wish to purchase.
For individual orders, turn to the back of the book for
more information.

Timelapse™

The Official Strategy Guide

Rick Barba

Prima Publishing
Rocklin, California
(916) 632-4400

Project Editor: Julie Asbury

Important:
Prima Publishing has made every effort to determine that the information contained in this book is accurate. However, the publisher makes no warranty, either expressed or implied, as to the accuracy, effectiveness, or completeness of the material in this book; nor does the publisher assume liability for damages, either incidental or consequential, that may result from using the information in this book. The publisher cannot provide information regarding game play, hints and strategies, or problems with hardware or software. Questions should be directed to the support numbers provided by the game and device manufacturers in their documentation. Some game tricks require precise timing and may require repeated attempts before the desired result is achieved.

ISBN: 7615-0497-4
Library of Congress Catalog Card Number: 96-73072
Printed in the United States of America

96 97 98 99 BB 10 9 8 7 6 5 4 3 2 1
Visit us online at http://www.primapublishing.com

Contents

Foreword

Have you ever wished you could explore an ancient civilization like Egypt? Take a walk through the fabled lost city of Atlantis? Or be the first to unravel an amazing alien secret undiscovered for thousands of years? Well, now you can.

Timelapse is the culmination of two years of hard work by the combined efforts of a talented team of dedicated people. We wanted to create a game designed not only to entertain you, but also to challenge you, and perhaps even cause you to ask yourself, "What if this could have actually happened?"

We think we've succeeded. *Timelapse* features photo-realistic full-screen graphics, a wide variety of indigenous and challenging puzzles integrated into the story and worlds, and an intriguing storyline which blurs fact with fiction. As you travel through time and space, you will unravel the mystery of Atlantis and discover that its influence goes far beyond what you may have ever imagined.

Thank you for purchasing *Timelapse*. We appreciate your support and hope you will enjoy the journey as much as we enjoyed creating it for you. And now, Easter Island awaits you …

Lori Nichols
Lori Nichols
Producer

Mike Yuen
Mike Yuen
Product Marketing Manager

GTE Entertainment
Carlsbad, California
1996

Acknowledgments

Part of the joy of writing strategy guides is the opportunity to fully immerse oneself in some of the best computer games to hit the market each year. But for me, a far bigger joy is the opportunity to work with people like Lori Nichols, Mike Yuen, Mike Ward, Sal Parascandolo, and the rest of the GTE Entertainment team—people who not only designed a truly gorgeous and compelling game, but also found the time (despite their own crushing deadlines) to help make this book possible.

Thanks also to the Prima crew, especially Julie Asbury, whose sense of humor kept me sane and whose deft guidance kept everything on track; Sam Mills, whose editing acumen (which I envy) made the book's prose so much better; and Connie Nixon, whose elegant design for this book is one of the best I've ever seen. Special thanks also to Brett Skogen, who lured me onto the project before I'd even heard of *Timelapse,* and to Juliana Aldous and Debra Kempker, whose general support continues to make working for Prima Publishing one of the best gigs a writer could possibly have.

TIMELAPSE

Introduction

WELCOME TO THE OFFICIAL, fully authorized strategy guide for *Timelapse*. If you've played even a few sample minutes of the game, you know it's easily one of the most beautiful and intriguing experiences ever burned onto a CD-ROM. The stunning art, the atmosphere, the compelling story and its basis in archeological fact—all —combine to make *Timelapse* a worthy successor to the venerable game that inspired it and established its genre, *Myst*.

How to Use This Book

Whether you seek soft-serve hints or hard-boiled answers, you'll find exactly what you need here. But before we go any further, let's make one thing clear. This book assumes you've read the game documentation and you're familiar with the *Timelapse* interface. If this is not the case—well, get thee to a user manual.

"Part One: General Hints" is for people who prefer gentle nudges in the right direction to simple, spoon-fed answers. This section features "soft hints" in a question-and-answer format offering subtle clues for some of the game's tougher puzzles.

"Part Two: *Timelapse* Walkthrough" is a detailed, step-by-step solution path for the game. The walkthrough is divided into sections for each of the five *Timelapse* worlds—Easter Island, Egypt, Anasazi, Maya, and Atlantis. Each section offers not only quick solutions, but also explains the puzzle logic, when possible. Use this book's Contents to find the location or puzzle stumping you, then turn to that section to get all the answers you seek.

"Part Three: Interview with the *Timelapse* Team" offers a penetrating glimpse into the design process for this remarkable game. In August of 1996, shortly before the release of *Timelapse,* I spoke with members of the GTE Entertainment *Timelapse* team in a conference call to their headquarters in Carlsbad, California. This section documents that lively conversation.

The Opening

Timelapse opens with a breathtaking, low-altitude approach to Easter Island. You hear the voice of Professor Alexander Nichols—someone you know well, apparently—on your voice answering machine at home. His message is urgent, compelling … and somewhat disturbing.

> *I know I can count on you. You're the only one I trust. All my life I've believed there's a link between the ancient civilizations of the Egyptians, Mayans, the Anasazi, and the lost city of Atlantis. For the past twenty years I've traveled the globe in search of Atlantis. Through it all, I've endured the endless ridicule of my colleagues. Now, finally, I've found that missing link. Here on Easter Island I've discovered what appears to be some sort of alien device. In it I can see worlds from the past, brilliant scenes, flowing by like clouds. Whatever it is, it definitely is not man-made. If I am right, and this device is a time gate, then this may be the greatest archeological discovery of all time. Tomorrow I'll attempt to activate the time portal and go through it. I don't know what will happen to me when I try this. Please, hurry. I need your help. You must come at once to Easter Island. You're the only one I trust.*

And so the SGI-rendered, full-screen, high-resolution, photo-realistic, ray-traced, 3D adventure begins.

PART ONE

General Hints

IGH-LEVEL GOVERNMENT RESEARCH proves that people who buy strategy guides prefer straight answers to coy hints by a ratio of about 12,000,000 to 1. Unfortunately, that one guy writes a lot of nasty letters. In deference to him, I include this section. Here, you'll find hints that nudge you along the *Timelapse* solution path without giving you outright answers. Some of these hints are vague, some specific. Many emerge from lame attempts to amuse myself. The overriding impulse, however, is a noble desire to protect you from your cheatin' heart.

First, should I read all of the professor's journal when I arrive in each world? There are so many words.

▲ Yes.

Easter Island

What should I do first?

▲ Register for that math logic class down at the local community college.

▲ Clean your bedroom.

▲ Then explore the nearby pathways. Two important items lie within a few paces of your arrival point.

Is there anything important at the abandoned campsite?

▲ Anything that you can manipulate will be important.

▲ Click on everything and take what you can.

▲ Ever played "Paper, Rock, Scissors"? How does "rock" lose?

▲ Sketch a solution for yourself.

▲ Seek instructions to gain enlightenment.

I found a cave, but I can't get very far.

▲ Timelapse is too responsible to let players stumble around in the dark.

▲ Do you see a light source?

▲ That's probably the professor's lantern. Where would he keep the instructions for operating it?

Whenever I put the cave stone faces in the outstretched hands of the three cave statues, the stones crumble into sand. What am I doing wrong?

▲ You must put the correct cave stone in each of the six hands.

▲ Hands generally run up arms to shoulders. See anything there?

▲ Each cave stone is associated with a glyph in the eyes of the big lava-head that produced them.

▲ The cave stone glyphs correspond to the shoulder glyphs.

▲ Have you seen any pairs of glyphs elsewhere on the island?

▲ Check out the campsite and the waterfront path.

▲ Find the six glyph pairs—three on a *Rongorongo* board, three on a trio of *Moai* heads.

Egypt

How do I get into the pyramid?

▲ You need the combination for the tumbler lock on the door.

▲ The combination is on the other side of the Nile.

▲ Opening the pyramid door is the last puzzle in Egypt. You have a lot of work to do on the far side of the river first.

I know I need to use the boat to cross the river, but the stone dock is locked shut. How do I open it?

▲ Two words: Water weight.

▲ Did you examine the illustration at the bottom of the water spirit pool?

▲ Examine the stone trough, experiment with its components, and figure out their relationships.

▲ Did you find the basket that scoops Nile water into the trough?

▲ Too much water from the river spills the trough; too much water from the trough spills the well bucket.

▲ When filling the well bucket, make sure it's under the spout from the trough.

▲ But after the well bucket holds the proper water weight, look carefully at it again. What will happen if you lower it further?

▲ The final step takes place on the dock itself.

I made it to the other side of the river, but that crocodile won't let me pass.

▲ Kill it! Of course, you need a weapon first.

▲ Examine the barge for a weapon.

▲ The crocodile has only one soft spot. When you hit it, the croc reacts.

▲ You didn't think just one good hit would melt a magic crocodile, did you?

I found a cool bust with a crystal globe in the Dock Temple, but it doesn't do anything.

▲ Did you turn it on?

▲ The power source is nearby. Just listen.

I opened the chest in the storeroom and found an important-looking tablet. What does it mean?

▲ It's an inventory list.

▲ Do the items look familiar? They should. They're all around you.

▲ On the tablet, the Egyptian symbol next to each item is a number.

▲ Translate the numbers. Remember, this is an inventory of items—not only in this storeroom, but in the one on the other side of the Main Hall.

I'm in a chamber full of crystals. Each crystal has three glyphs I can set. How do I figure out the correct settings?

▲ The top glyph is a particular god. Match the god to its background color.

▲ Did you carefully examine all the obelisks outside?

▲ The middle glyph is the god's special number.

▲ Check the obelisks again, but do the math, too.

▲ The math is on the warrior's scroll in the Temple storeroom.

▲ The bottom glyph is the god's secret symbol. Carefully watch the rolling globe back in the Temple.

I got past the cobra, but the corridor ends at a well. I can see retracted stairs in the well walls. How do I get them out?

▲ Push the button.

▲ But power up the mechanism first.

▲ Remember the power source?

I got the Gene Pod! But what's this scroll with the pyramid drawing mean?

▲ "Where you find the scarab, you find the key."

▲ What sort of thing often needs a key?

▲ OK, OK … this is the combination to the Pyramid door lock.

But all I see is columns of symbols. How do I translate the combination?

▲ When you turn the tumbler wheels in the Pyramid door lock, what do you see? Egyptian numbers, right?

▲ Four columns on the tablet, four tumblers in the lock. Figure it out.

I got the right combination entered in the Pyramid tumbler lock, and I clicked on the triangle button to open the door ... but nothing happens! What did I do wrong?

▲ Did you power up the door mechanism first?

▲ Surely you know the power source by now.

Maya

I got past the chameleon into the Castillo Pyramid, but I'm stumped by this 3-by-4 tile grid. How does it work?

▲ Things really add up in this puzzle, from top to bottom.

▲ Each tile in the bottom row is a sum.

▲ To translate the dots and dashes into numbers, check the professor's journal.

It's fun rolling this crystal globe around the morphing bust, but what exactly am I doing?

▲ Each morphing head and its corresponding glyph (in the globe) should look familiar if you were observant on the path up from the beach.

▲ Roll the globe over a glyph, then check out the stelae on the beach path. Which one is different now?

I activated a stele and pressed its button. Three glyphs lit up. Now what?

▲ Go back to the Castillo Pyramid and find the glyphs.

▲ Line them up on the Mayan calendar wheels.

… which is easier said than done. Is there a foolproof method for lining up the Mayan calendar wheels?

▲ Yes.

▲ To learn it, purchase at least twenty copies of *Timelapse: The Official Strategy Guide,* line them up end to end, and then …

▲ Just kidding. But a foolproof four-step method for the Mayan calendar wheel is described in the "Maya" chapter in Part Two of this book.

Why can't I get into any of the other buildings beyond the Castillo Pyramid?

▲ You have to unlock them with the Mayan calendar wheel.

I can't get past the stone idol blocking the jungle path.

▲ Find him some eyes.

▲ You'll find both nearby—look for the glint.

This crystal pyramid puzzle in the Lizard Temple seems impossible! How can I light the 22 tiers in just 22 moves?

▲ Don't feel bad. Few people could do it without help.

▲ Apparently, you didn't find the solution parchment on the floor across the room.

▲ Red is left, black is right.

I got the Gene Pod, but now I'm trapped by stalactites! How do I get out of here?

▲ When the podium went up, the stalactite gate came down.

▲ Lower the podium to its original height to raise the gate.

I got past the stone idol down the jungle path to the Sun Temple, but I can't get in.

▲ You can't enter the Sun Temple until you've found and placed all four of the jewels in their respective temples.

▲ You also need a fifth jewel for the center of the Sun Temple door.

▲ You passed the fifth jewel on the jungle path.

▲ To palm the jewel, you need a big head.

How do I know what the slider puzzle in the Sun Temple should look like when it's done?

▲ Did you pay attention after each of the four messages from Mayan priests?

▲ The wall disks in each of the four temples show the final images.

▲ The wall disks also include clues to the placement of each image in the slider puzzle.

▲ Look closely at the slider puzzle's border

Anasazi

What's with this snake painting and all the animal footprints?

▲ If you move from the first circle on the snake (by its head) to the next circle, which direction are you going?

▲ Each animal footprint under the snake represents a direction.

I found a lever that moves a big rock mechanism. What is it doing?

▲ Directing power to other mechanisms in the area.

▲ Activating one mechanism deactivates the others.

But where are these other mechanisms?

▲ After you move the lever to each position, look behind the rock mechanism.

▲ Seen that symbol anywhere else?

This flashlight won't work.

▲ Come on. What do you do with a balky flashlight?

▲ Read the journal. How did the professor get it to work?

The squirrel dropped his acorn, but I can't get it out of the rock.

▲ You need a stick.

▲ Actually, you need a sticky stick.

This feather headdress puzzle is fun, but I can't seem to find all the feathers.

▲ Get off the beaten track.

▲ Only four of the headdress feathers are in the North Rock area.

▲ The quail feather is under a bush not far away.

At last! Something to shoot! But my arrows fly wildly to the side of the target—and well short, too.

▲ To shoot straight, your arrow needs an arrowhead.

▲ To shoot with enough distance, your arrow needs a boost.

▲ What did the shaman's voice tell you? "Shoot straight as the wind blows."

▲ Listen to the wind for a minute or so. Hear a pattern?

These four stone tablets look important, but nothing much happens when I mess with them.

▲ Nothing happens until you solve the puzzles at the four locations represented by the sun spirals at the top of the tablets.

But I solved the puzzles at the other four locations!

▲ Like the puzzles at the other rock formations, the four-tablets puzzle must be activated.

▲ Note the sun spiral above the tablets—no sun dagger.

▲ Which lever setting back at the rock formation matches that?

The four tablets are covered with glyphs. Which ones do I click on?

▲ Note the top of each tablet.

▲ Each tablet contains two active glyphs that correspond to your experience at the location indicated by the tablet's sun spiral.

▲ One active glyph represents your "spirit guide" at each location. (Read the professor's journal to learn what form these guides take.)

▲ The other active glyph represents a sound.

▲ Did you pay attention in the secret chambers at each of the other puzzles?

How do I get up to the cliff dwelling?

▲ Think Jack and the Cornstalk.

▲ Water the ear of corn.

▲ You don't need to haul the water—it's right there.

▲ A nearby utensil will help release the water.

How do I get past the snake to the ladder?

▲ Click on the snake and listen carefully.

▲ The snake just wants to be flattered.

▲ Imitation is the best form of flattery.

What do I do in the loom room?

▲ Finish that blanket on the loom.

▲ String yarn through the loom with the shuttle stick.

▲ Pull the damper to weave the stringed yarn.

▲ To complete the blanket, use the yarn balls in the correct order.

I got into the kiva, and I'm surrounded by glyphs that light up when I touch them. Which ones do I push?

▲ Just the ones you've seen elsewhere.

▲ Push the seven glyphs you discovered at the other puzzles.

▲ Don't forget the one on the Gene Pod.

Atlantis

Why do I get that annoying buzz every time I push the Atlantis button on a time gate device?

▲ You can't go to Atlantis until you've found all three of the Gene Pods.

How do I activate the elevator in the building at the center of the complex?

▲ You must visit the other four buildings first.

▲ Each of the outer buildings contains a wealth of information—and an elevator "key."

▲ Find the correct glyph for each of the building icons on the elevator control panel.

The Guardian nails me every time I grab his crystal.

▲ You're not moving fast enough.

The Guardian nails me on the upper level in the stasis room.

▲ You're not moving fast enough.

How am I supposed to figure out the stasis pod activation code?

▲ It's all around you.

▲ Check the other stasis pods.

How can I get the Guardian into the stasis pod?

▲ You need bait.

▲ Do you have anything that belongs to him?

▲ Once he arrives, give him an energetic nudge into the pod. (You finally get to blast something!)

▲ Once he's in the pod, "hit" the activation button.

I gave the Genetic Device to the professor like he said, and things went haywire!

▲ Would you jump off a cliff if he asked you to?

▲ Remember the video warning about "home world metals" that destroy time gates?

Journal entry:
I'm on my way to Easter
Island. Finally I have time
to summarize my notes. I'm

Arrival

Moai "Trio"

Campsite

CHAPTER 1
Easter Island

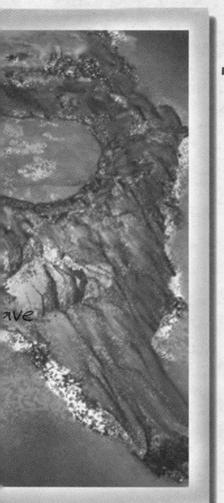

ave

TIMELAPSE'S EASTER ISLAND is beautiful, isn't it? But don't let its tranquil surface fool you. Under this windswept seascape beats a powerful geothermal heart, pumping pools of magma and superheated water through a webwork of underground caves. Easter Island is the game's smallest world by far, featuring only two puzzles of consequence. But here you'll find Professor Nichols' journal and, more importantly (for those hardy few who don't use strategy guides), his instant camera. Your goal is to gain access to a mysterious time portal hidden somewhere on the island.

Arrival: Lakeside Path

After the introductory sequence, you arrive on the rim of an extinct volcano on an uninhabited section of the island. Before you juts an outcropping of rocks covered with strange bird carvings. A lake fills the dead volcano's crater just behind the outcropping.

FIGURE 1-1. EASTER ARRIVAL. HERE'S WHERE YOU START YOUR *TIMELAPSE* ADVENTURE.

▲ Turn right to face up the lakeside path. You should see a bird hop off a rock and fly away. (Clue!)

▲ Move forward two times up the path and turn right to face the rock.

▲ Move forward to get a close-up of the instant camera.

FIGURE 1-2. INSTANT CAMERA. TO COMPLETE *TIMELAPSE* WITH A MINIMUM OF OUTSIDE HELP (FROM ME, FOR EXAMPLE), NAB THIS CAMERA.

- ▲ Take the camera.

- ▲ Move back a step and turn right.

- ▲ Go forward two times (back to Arrival).

- ▲ Turn left to face up the Beach Path.

Beach Path: Professor's Journal

- ▲ Go forward five times, then turn right to face the *Moai* stone statue.

- ▲ Step forward to the *Moai* statue. Notice the journal on the ground?

FIGURE 1-3. ADVENTURER'S BIBLE. DON'T MISS THIS LITTLE ITEM. PROFESSOR NICHOLS LEFT IT HERE JUST BEFORE HE WAS TRAPPED IN THE TIME GATE IN ATLANTIS. BE SURE TO GRAB IT.

▲ Click on the journal. This puts it in your inventory.

▲ Optional: Press [Control] + [J] to open the journal (or ⌘ + [J] in Macintosh version).

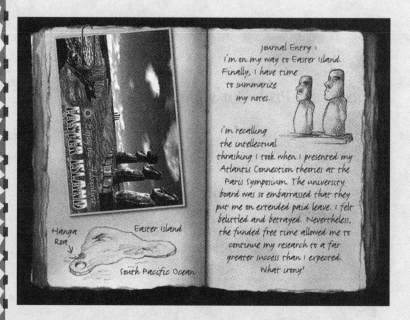

FIGURE 1-4. GOOD READ. THE PROFESSOR'S JOURNAL HOLDS A WEALTH OF TANTALIZING INFORMATION AND FILLS IN THE GAME HISTORY QUITE NICELY.

I strongly recommend you read the entire journal at this point. You learn all of the back story—the professor's discovery of "commonalities" between the great ancient cultures, including evidence of common genetic advancement, and his belief in the existence of Atlantis. Nichols also chronicles his discovery of an aging shaman who tells fabulous tales of mysterious "Great Ones."

▲ Optional: Click on either the right or left page to close the journal

Let's follow the Beach Path down to the ocean:

▲ Back away from the stone statue and turn left to face down the Beach Path.

▲ Go forward four times and turn left.

▲ Go forward seven times and turn right.

▲ Go forward four times and turn left.

▲ Go forward five times to the edge of the water—a pair of curious crabs cross the rocks when you arrive—and turn right.

▲ Go forward two times, then turn right. You should face the rightmost of three *Moai* statues that look out to the ocean.

FIGURE 1-5. WE THREE KINGS. EXAMINE THESE THREE *MOAI* STATUES CAREFULLY. EACH HAS SOMETHING IMPORTANT TO GET OFF ITS CHEST.

Beach Path: Three *Moai* Statues

▲ Note the glyph at the base of the first statue.

▲ Step forward to the first statue and click on its chest to see another glyph.

▲ Repeat these two steps with the other two *Moai* statues.

To minimize your use of this strategy guide, either sketch the glyph pairs or press [Control] + [C] (or [⌘] + [C] in Macintosh version) and snap photos of each glyph for later reference: You may take a maximum of 36 shots in the game. Note, if you decide not to take a picture, simply drag the view-finder to the bottom of the screen.

FIGURE 1-6. GLYPH PARTNERS. EACH STATUE IN THE MOAI TRIO HAS ONE GLYPH INSCRIBED ON ITS BASE AND ANOTHER ON THE CHEST. HERE'S THE GLYPH PAIR FROM THE RIGHTMOST *MOAI* STATUE.

▲ After you produce the glyph on the chest of the last (left-most) statue, back away from the statue and turn right.

▲ Go forward 10 times to reach Professor Nichols' campsite.

FIGURE 1-7. CAMP NICHOLS. HERE'S THE PROFESSOR'S STUFF.
EXAMINE EVERYTHING, AND TAKE WHAT YOU CAN.
BELIEVE ME, HE WON'T MIND.

Campsite

▲ Move straight ahead as far as possible to get a close-up of the wooden *Rongorongo* board on the table.

▲ Pick up the piece of paper in the lower right corner.

▲ Drag the paper over the *Rongorongo* board.

▲ Pick up the pencil and touch it on the paper to make an imprint of the *Rongorongo* board.

FIGURE 1-8. RIGHT OR *RONGORONGO?* THOSE THREE PAIRS OF GLYPHS SURE STAND OUT, DON'T THEY?

Note that three pairs of glyphs are darker than the others. Remember the paired glyphs on the three *Moai* statues down the beach? Add these *Rongorongo* glyphs to those *Moai* glyphs, and you have six pairs of glyphs. Do you think these will be significant later? If you don't, stop now and resign yourself to abject failure in the computer age.

▲ Back up two times and turn right to face the side table.

▲ Move forward to get a close-up of the items on the side table.

▲ Click on the matchbox (lower right) to pick it up. It now occupies an inventory position in the corner of the screen.

▲ Click on the sheet of gas-lantern instructions for a close-up. You can't take it, but read it carefully.

FIGURE 1-9. OBJECT OF ENLIGHTENMENT. THIS LITTLE BOX WILL BRIGHTEN UP YOUR DAY. TAKE IT.

▲ Back away one step from the table and turn right.

▲ Take one step forward (toward the ocean) and turn left. You should see a yellow-striped barrel and a tent stake at the left of the screen.

▲ Go forward three steps to the wall and turn right.

Hidden Cave Path

▲ Go forward seven steps to the blowhole where water shoots up through the rocks. Behind it lies a hidden cave.

▲ Go forward seven more steps to the mouth of the cave.

FIGURE 1-10. CAVE MOUTH. COULD THIS BE THE "DRIPPING CAVE" THE PROFESSOR MENTIONS IN HIS JOURNAL?

"Dripping Cave": Lighting the Lantern

▲ Enter the cave and go forward to the hanging lantern.

▲ Click on the lantern for a close-up.

Remember the instructions for the gas lantern? For your convenience, they appear next to a shot of the lantern itself in Figure 1-11.

FIGURE 1-11. LANTERN AND INSTRUCTIONS. HERE'S HOW TO USE AND ENJOY YOUR COLLINS GAS LANTERN.

First, you need to pump the tank. Here's how:

▲ Click and hold on the tank pump.

▲ Drag the pump up, then back down to pump the tank once. (or until you hear "hits"). Make sure the pump is down.

▲ Pump 10 times.

▲ Open the primer valve. To do so, click on it once to flip it up.

▲ Click twice on the gas knob to move it to the "on" position (arrow pointing up).

▲ Click and hold on the matchbox to take a single match.

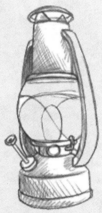

Note
Pump the lantern at least 10 times.

If you release the mouse button, the match drops! But if you drop a match, just get another one. The matchbox holds an unlimited supply.

FIGURE 1-12. SUCCESSFUL STRIKE. TO LIGHT A MATCH, SIMPLY CLICK ON THE BOX TO GET A MATCH, THEN DRAG THE MATCH ACROSS THE FLINT ON THE BOX'S SIDE.

▲ Drag the match along the flint on the side of the matchbox. This lights the match.

▲ Move the lit match to the lantern's mantle. This lights the lantern.

▲ Click on the primer valve to flip it down, closing the valve again.

"Dripping Cave": Morphing Cave Stones Puzzle

▲ Back away from the lantern close-up, then move forward 13 times, until you reach a dead end marked by a stone face carving.

▲ Turn left and move forward three times (just past the skull on the cave floor).

▲ Turn left and move forward twice to see the "lava tongue" extend from the big stone face.

FIGURE 1-13.
MIGHTY MORPHIN'
LAVA-HEADS. AFTER
THE STONE FACE
REGURGITATES LAVA,
NOTE THE GLYPH IN ITS
EYES. LOOK FAMILIAR?
IT SHOULD—IT'S THE
SAME GLYPH YOU
FOUND ON THE CHEST
OF A *MOAI* STATUE.

A small cave stone head rises from the lava tongue, and a glyph appears in the statue's eyes. Click repeatedly on the eyes to rotate them. As the eyes rotate, the glyph changes; each new glyph prompts a new cave stone to rise from the tongue. Notice how you can scroll through six different cave stones, each with its own corresponding eye-glyph. Note also that you've seen each glyph before—three on the *Rongorongo* board and three on the chests of the *Moai* statues on the Beach Path.

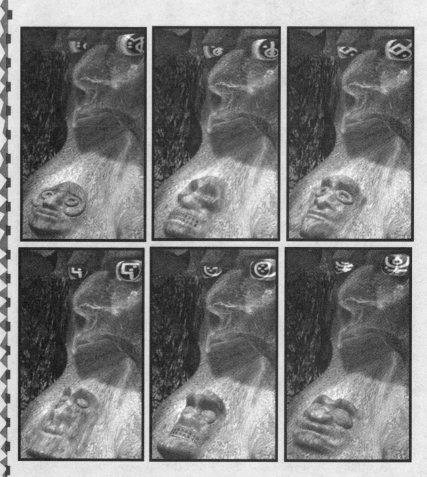

FIGURE 1-14. STONES AND GLYPHS. ROTATE THE STATUE'S
EYES TO SCROLL THROUGH THE GLYPHS.
EACH GLYPH TRIGGERS THE RISE OF A
DIFFERENT CAVE STONE FROM THE LAVA TONGUE.

Those cave stones are pretty hot, being lava and all. Maybe
we should lower their temperature a bit before we take one.
For the sake of order, let's start by rotating the eye-glyphs all
the way to the left.

▲ Keep clicking on the left eye until it stops changing. (In the eye, you should see a glyph that looks like a reversed dollar sign; on the tongue, you should see a cave stone head that looks like Charlie Brown on a particularly bad day.)

▲ Click on the stone bowl just to the left of the big stone face.

▲ After the water pours, wait a couple of seconds, then click on the cooled cave stone to take it. (Don't dally, though. The cave stone stays cool for only a few seconds.) Once you officially nab the stone, it moves to the corner of your screen.

FIGURE 1-15. HOW TO GET A HEAD. FIRST, COOL IT OFF WITH A SHOT OF COLD WATER. THEN GRAB IT FAST, BEFORE IT HEATS UP AGAIN.

Note
You can take the cave stone heads in any order, but only one at a time. You can also replace a cooled cave stone back on the lava tongue.

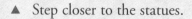

▲ Once you get a cave stone, back away from the stone face and turn twice to face the three Atlantean god statues.

▲ Step closer to the statues.

Two things stand out when you look at the Atlantean god statues. Each god has both hands extended, and each has a pair of glyphs on its shoulders. Again, the six shoulder glyphs should look familiar—three from the *Rongorongo* board, three from the bases of the three *Moai* statues back on the beach.

FIGURE 1-16. WILL WORK FOR HEADS.
CLEARLY, THESE GUYS ARE LOOKING FOR A HANDOUT.
WHAT SORT OF THING WOULD A GOD WANT?

As you may have guessed, you must place the six cooled cave stones, one at a time, in the hands of the three Atlantean

god statues. You also need to place them in the correct order. I'll explain the logic and give a step-by-step solution below. If you're impatient and want a quick solution, jump ahead to Figure 1-17 to see the final configuration.

Step-by-Step Solution: How to Place the Cave Stones

1. Cool a cave stone and take it from the lava tongue.

2. Before you turn away, note the glyph in the eye of the stone face.

3. Match this "cave stone glyph" with its partner "Atlantean glyph" found on the shoulder of one of the Atlantean god statues.

4. Place the cave stone in the hand that extends from the shoulder with the matching glyph.

   Remember that three glyph partners appear on the *Rongorongo* board back at the campsite, and the other three glyph pairs appear on the three *Moai* statues on the Beach Path.

Note
If you place any cave stone in the wrong hand, all previously placed cave stones crumble into sand. Fortunately, the lava tongue reproduces cave stones endlessly, so you can go back, grab a new stone, and start over without loading a saved game.

TABLE 4-1 TABLE OF MATCHING GLYPHS
Pair Found On:

Rongorongo	*Rongorongo*	*Rongorongo*	Left *Moai*	Middle *Moai*	Right *Moai*
Cave Stone Glyph					
Glyph 1A	Glyph 2A	Glyph 3A	Glyph 4A	Glyph 5A	Glyph 6A
Atlantean Glyph					
Glyph 1B	Glyph 2B	Glyph 3B	Glyph 4B	Glyph 5B	Glyph 6B

FIGURE 1-17. HEAD & SHOULDERS. FOR YOU
QUICK-SOLUTION LOVERS, HERE'S THE CORRECT
ORDER OF CAVE STONE PLACEMENT.

"Dripping Cave": *Makemake* Door

Once you've placed the heads in the correct order, take the following steps:

▲ Back away from the stone gods.

▲ Turn left and step forward to the rock door with the *Makemake* (face) painting with glowing eyes.

The professor's journal tells you that cave stones were used as "keys" to open secret Rapa Nui caves, and the face of *Makemake* protects those caves from intruders.

▲ Click on the face painting and watch it dissolve into an open portal.

FIGURE 1-18. *MAKEMAKE* DOOR. IF YOU PLACED ALL SIX CAVE STONES PROPERLY, THIS DOOR OPENS WITH A SIMPLE CLICK.

Time Gate: Transportal Room

Step forward seven times to the orb and watch the image of Professor Nichols appear in the swirling nebula. Could this be the mysterious "Chanting Light" he mentioned in his journal? You bet it could. Nichols makes his speech from the orb only once, so here's a transcript for you:

> Thank God, you've come at last! My situation is desperate. I'm trapped, imprisoned in this timeless dimension. You must have found my journal, my camera. Did you see the photographs I took? They are few, I know, but study them. They prove the wondrous discoveries I made are real. And far beyond even my wildest dreams.
>
> This won't be easy to understand. I don't fully comprehend it myself. But this device is a transportal—a gate through time itself. I learned to travel freely among these ancient worlds. And so can you. For 20 years I've theorized a link between the ancient civilizations, much to the amusement of my colleagues. Now, my life's work will be vindicated. Please, do your best to reach me. You will come to believe the unbelievable—not only about the ancients, but about the very nature of mankind.

FIGURE 1-19. DR. NICHOLS, I PRESUME? YES, AND THE PROFESSOR IS SO VERY HAPPY TO SEE YOU.

If you wait a few seconds, you get one more message from Professor Nichols:

> *I've theorized about time travel, of course, and considered it impossible—well beyond any present or future technology. How ironic that I should stumble upon it at an archeological site. As I pondered the origin of the time gates, I began to see truth in the mythology of the past.*

How to Use the Time Gate

Five illustrated buttons on the base of the orb activate passage to the five locations to which you can travel in the game. Counterclockwise from left, the buttons represent Egypt, Anasazi, Atlantis, Maya, and Easter Island. Click on a button to trigger a spinning animation of that destination within the orb. Note, however, that you can't access Atlantis yet.

Egypt

Anasazi   Atlantis   Maya   Easter Island

FIGURE 1-20. SPACE–TIME DISCONTINUUM. CLICK ON THE BUTTONS TO SEE SPINNING 360-DEGREE SHOTS OF FOUR DESTINATIONS. (ATLANTIS, THE CENTER BUTTON, DOESN'T WORK YET.) CLICK ON THE ACTIVE ANIMATION IN THE ORB TO TRAVEL TO THAT SPOT.

▲ Click on the leftmost button—the one with the scarab beetle. You'll see an animation of ancient Egypt in the orb.

▲ Click on the orb to travel to Egypt.

Bonus: Easter Island Easter Egg

From your Easter Island arrival point, turn 180 degrees and follow the path past the *Moai* head where you found the journal. When you reach the first turn in the path—that is, you can't go forward any farther—make a 180-degree turn to look back at the *Moai* head at the top of the hill. Hold down Control (or ⌘ in the Macintosh version) and click on the head.

FIGURE 1-21. HERE'S YOUR HAT, WHAT'S YOUR HURRY?
HOLD DOWN Control, CLICK ON THAT HEAD, AND WATCH.

Egypt—a land of order and
linear formality ...

Pyramid

Mount
(to Cv

Water
spirit Pool
Arrival

Boat
Dock

Dock
Temple

CHAPTER 2
Egypt

ACCORDING TO THE DESIGNERS' HANDBOOK, the Egypt of *Timelapse* is "a land of order and linear formality." The floor plan divides it into two areas, one on each bank of the Nile River. The puzzles offer a nice mix of logic, information gathering, and chance games. Most of the puzzles feature elements of Egyptian culture. Before you get started, I highly recommend you press Control + J (or ⌘ + J in Macintosh version) to open the professor's journal and read the new Egypt pages available to you.

West Bank: Arrival

You arrive in Egypt on the west side of the Nile River. The most efficient solution path—say, the one you'd use if you were cheating—leads from your arrival point directly across the Nile to the east shore. But how do you cross the river? Yes, there's a boat on the bank. But the vessel is locked into a stone dock. Let's seek clues before we try our hand at recreational boating.

FIGURE 2-1. EGYPT ARRIVAL. UPON ARRIVAL IN EGYPT, YOUR NATURAL INCLINATION WOULD BE TO CLIMB THE HILL TO THIS GORGEOUS POOL. TRUST YOURSELF.

Water Spirit Pool

▲ Climb the hill to the pool.

▲ Watch the water spirit rise and speak: "Glory to the wind, for it is her breath that escorts you across the Nile." Good to know.

▲ Go forward three times to see the illustration at the bottom of the pool.

FIGURE 2-2. SPIRITED WATER. HER MESSAGE SEEMS TO BE, "CROSS THE RIVER, CHECK IT OUT." IS SHE WITH THE TRAVEL BUREAU?

The pool illustration provides a serious clue about the steps necessary to get the boat across the Nile. Snap a photo with your instant camera, if you want (but I'll insert the illustration later when we check out the boat dock).

▲ Move back three times and turn right to face the Pyramid.

▲ Go forward five times and turn left to face the Pharaoh statue. (My designers' notes call it a "lawn jockey," but I don't think so.) A voice says, "Where you find the scarab, you find the key."

Oooh, cryptic. At this point, you can continue down the path and enter the Pyramid. But you won't get far inside. To reach the heart of the ancient structure, you must unlock the door. To unlock the door, you must learn the tumbler lock's four-glyph combination. That, as you might expect, lies hidden on the east bank of the Nile.

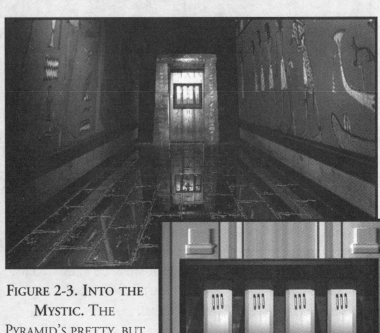

FIGURE 2-3. INTO THE MYSTIC. THE PYRAMID'S PRETTY, BUT IT'S A DEAD END (NO PUN INTENDED) RIGHT NOW. COME BACK LATER WHEN YOU FIND THE COMBINATION TO THAT TUMBLER LOCK.

▲ Retrace your steps to the spot where you arrived in Egypt.

▲ Continue down the path to the stone trough near the boat dock.

Boat Dock Puzzle

The object of this puzzle is to free the Egyptian barge and sail to the other side of the Nile. A gate locks the barge in to the stone dock. A rope runs from the gate to a bucket hanging in a stone well. The idea is to fill the well bucket with water so its weight pulls the rope, opening the dock gate. Of course, you have some levers to flip, too. What self-respecting puzzle wouldn't have levers?

Before you start, let's take a look at the illustration from the bottom of the water spirit pool.

FIGURE 2-4. POOL CUE. THIS ILLUSTRATION AT THE BOTTOM OF THE POOL OFFERS A CLUE TO THE BOAT PUZZLE SOLUTION—FOUR BASKETS OF WATER, PULL LEVER 1, TWO BASKETS OF WATER, PULL LEVER 1, THEN PULL LEVER 2.

The top of the illustration depicts four containers pouring water, then a lever (marked by one dot) being pulled. Below that you see two more containers pouring water, then the same lever pulled again. Finally, we see a second lever (marked by two dots) pulled to the left, followed by a depiction of an opening gate. Got it?

Now let's get to work. You should be at the edge of the stone trough:

▲ Turn right to face the river and step forward to the water's edge.

▲ Turn left to face a basket hanging on a rope.

FIGURE 2-5. WATER BASKET. CLICK ON THIS BASKET TO SCOOP WATER INTO THE STONE TROUGH. SCOOP MORE THAN FOUR BASKETS, THOUGH, AND THE TROUGH EMPTIES BACK INTO THE RIVER.

Again, remember the pool illustration. It shows four baskets of water, then a lever pull, then two more baskets of water. Why? Because it takes the weight of six baskets of water in the well bucket to open the gate. But the trough that feeds water to the well bucket can hold only four baskets of water at a time; any more, and it empties back into the river. So try this:

▲ Click on the basket to scoop water into the trough.

▲ Repeat this step three more times (and no more!) for a total of four baskets of water scooped into the trough.

▲ Once you've scooped four baskets of water, return to the path and move down the trough to the pair of levers (see Figure 2-6).

FIGURE 2-6. LEVER ACTION. THE TOP LEVER MOVES THE WELL BUCKET. THE BOTTOM LEVER OPENS THE TROUGH SPOUT.

If you step forward to the levers, you can look down the well and see the bucket you must fill. Note that it isn't directly under the spout. You'll have to do something to correct that.

▲ Click on the top lever to flip it up. This moves the well bucket under the spout (Figure 2-7).

▲ Click on the bottom lever to open the spout. The four baskets of water from the trough rush into the bucket.

FIGURE 2-7. FILL POSITION. FLIP UP THE TOP LEVER TO
MOVE THE WELL BUCKET DIRECTLY UNDER
THE TROUGH SPOUT.

▲ Go back around the stone trough and scoop up two more baskets of water.

▲ Return to the levers.

▲ Make sure the top lever is still in the up position.

▲ Click on the bottom lever to open the spout again.

Two more baskets of water rush into the well bucket. You now have six baskets of water in the bucket—enough weight to pull the dock gate open and free the boat for river travel. But look into the well. See how the bucket teeters precariously on the ledge? If you go down the dock and release the dock lever, the bucket will spill and you'll have to start all over again.

FIGURE 2-8. ON THE EDGE. YIKES! THE BUCKET'S FULL. FLIP THE TOP LEVER DOWN AGAIN.

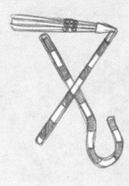

▲ Click on the top-left lever to flip it down. This moves the well bucket off the ledge.

▲ Go to the end of the dock and approach the dock lever.

▲ Pull the dock lever to the left to open the gate.

FIGURE 2-9. GATE UP. PUSH THE DOCK LEVER LEFT TO RAISE THE GATE.

▲ Board at the rear of the barge and move forward through the cabin toward the bow. This triggers the launch sequence.

▲ Ride the barge to the opposite shore.

East Bank: Getting Past the Crocodile

Your arrival on the east bank is greatly anticipated. Unfortunately, the anticipator is a crocodile—a magic one, at that. The creature morphs up at the end of the boat ramp and refuses to let you pass. This sort of intransigence must be punished—by death!

▲ Go directly back to the boat.

▲ Grab the spear leaning on the cabin. You now wield the deadly weapon.

▲ Return to the crocodile.

FIGURE 2-10. SPEAR HERE. GRAB THIS WEAPON. THEN GO MAKE MAGIC KABOBS OUT OF THAT PESKY CROCODILE.

Time for battle. When face-to-face with the crocodile, click the mouse to jab the spear forward. Cool! The crocodile is vulnerable on its right side in the lower neck and armpit area. Use the following combat tactics:

FIGURE 2-11. HIT THE SOFT SPOT. POSITION YOUR SPEAR AS SHOWN HERE, THEN JAB WHEN THE CROCODILE BOBS ITS HEAD TO THE LEFT, EXPOSING ITS "SOFT SPOT."

▲ First, position the spear as in Figure 2-11.

▲ Click to jab the spear when the crocodile moves its head to the left, exposing its "soft spot"—the neck/armpit area. (When you hit the right spot, the crocodile tosses his head in pain.)

▲ Stab the crocodile three times in its soft spot.

▲ After the crocodile melts into spirit soup, the spear disappears when you step forward.

Temple: *Main Hall*

The Temple consists of three rooms. You're in the *Main Hall,*
an open area lined by ornate pillars. Two enclosed rooms
extend to either side of the hall.

▲ From the spot where you killed the crocodile, move forward four times and turn left. See that glow behind the
pillar on the left?

▲ Go forward, then turn around. You should see a control
panel on the far right pillar.

**FIGURE 2-12. POWER
PILLAR.** THIS
BUZZING CONDUIT
CONTROLS THE
DISTRIBUTION OF
POWER TO THREE
EGYPTIAN PUZZLE
MECHANISMS.

Clearly, this is a power source. Each of the three buttons
on the panel's left directs power to a corresponding puzzle
mechanism in *Timelapse*'s Egyptian world. You can activate
only one mechanism at a time.

▲ Click on the panel's bottom button. This activates the Metamorphosis God puzzle key.

▲ Go forward, turn left, then approach the pedestal for a close-up of the bust of the Egyptian god.

FIGURE 2-13. UP ON A PEDESTAL. THIS GUY LOOKS IMPORTANT. BETTER TAKE A CLOSER LOOK.

Metamorphosis God Puzzle Key

This mechanism is easy to operate, and it yields much crucial information. Drag the crystal globe from left to right to magnify the eight Egyptian deity symbols. As the globe rolls in front of each god symbol, two things happen:

1. The bust transforms into the Egyptian deity represented by the symbol.

2. A "secret symbol" flashes in the crystal when the god's symbol is centered in the globe.

Note carefully the associations between the gods and their secret symbols. Below you'll find the corresponding elements—bust, symbol, and secret symbol—for each of the eight Egyptian deities:

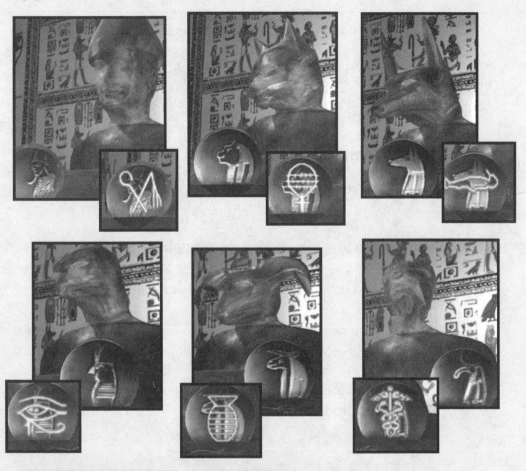

FIGURE 2-14. EGYPTIAN GODS
AND THEIR SECRET SYMBOLS

Tip
To save travel time later, go over to the power pillar now and click on the middle button, the one etched with the stairs icon.

53

OK, you've done all you can do in the *Main Hall*. Time to explore the side rooms.

▲ Back two steps away from the pedestal.

▲ Turn left and proceed through the doorway into the next room.

Temple: North Storeroom

▲ Turn to the dog statue and click on it. A voice cries out, "Seek the tablet!"

▲ Go past the dog statue and approach the baskets.

▲ Take the Mirror of Hathor out of its basket.

Click on the mirror and drag it around the screen to look at things—whoa, it's an X-ray viewer! Take a step back and use the mirror to read the snippety secret message on the wall: "You shall not leave the Temple storeroom without replacing the Mirror of Hathor."

FIGURE 2-15. MIRROR OF HATHOR. TAKE THE MIRROR FROM THE BASKET AND LOOK AT STUFF. IT'S GREAT FUN, AND QUITE REVEALING, TOO. SEE THAT KEY?

▲ Turn right to face the pottery.

▲ Use the Mirror of Hathor to look inside the pots until you find a key. (It's in the second pot from the right.)

▲ Leave the mirror over the pot with the key.

▲ Click on the key to take it.

The key moves to the corner of the screen and the Mirror of Hathor automatically returns to its basket. So we have a key. Now let's find something that needs unlocking.

- ▲ Turn right to face the ornate chest.

- ▲ Drag the key over the chest's lock and release it to unlock the chest.

- ▲ Move forward to get a top-down view of the chest.

- ▲ Click on the chest to open the lid.

- ▲ Click on the tablet beside the mummified head for a close-up. Be sure to drag your mouse over the head's eyes.

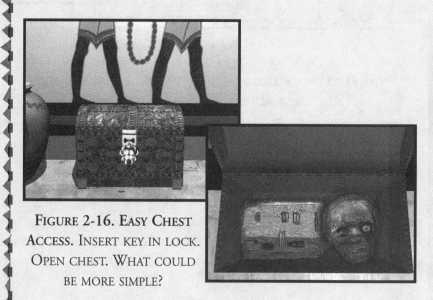

FIGURE 2-16. EASY CHEST ACCESS. INSERT KEY IN LOCK. OPEN CHEST. WHAT COULD BE MORE SIMPLE?

Egyptian Numbers Puzzle

The tablet is an ancient inventory of the items stored in the Dock Temple. The pictures stand for particular items, and the symbol next to each picture is an Egyptian number. To translate the Egyptian number symbols, count the number of items in the Dock Temple corresponding to each picture.

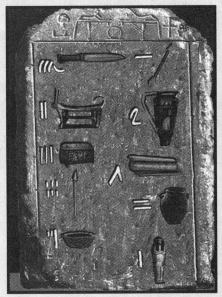

FIGURE 2-17. COUNT LIKE AN EGYPTIAN. THE TABLET IS AN INVENTORY LIST, SO THOSE SYMBOLS MUST BE EGYPTIAN NUMBERS.

Here's an example:

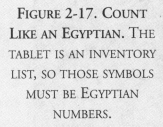

▲ On the tablet, note the symbol—a single horizontal line—next to the picture of the arrow.

▲ Put the tablet back in the chest, back away, and turn right.

▲ Go forward, left, forward to get a close-up of the arrows on the floor.

▲ Count the arrows. There are four.

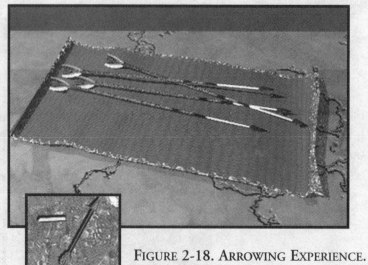

FIGURE 2-18. ARROWING EXPERIENCE.
TO TRANSLATE THE EGYPTIAN NUMERAL
NEXT TO THE ARROW ON THE INVENTORY TABLET,
COUNT THE NUMBER OF ARROWS IN THE
STOREROOM—IN THIS CASE, FOUR.

Now you know the horizontal line is the Egyptian symbol for the number four. Continue this process with the other items on the inventory list. If you explore the entire Temple, you find 10 scrolls, nine knives, eight large pots, seven ceramic pitchers, six spears, five baskets, four arrows, three ornate chests, two dog-eared tables, one sarcophagus, and a partridge in a pear tree.

The numbers translate like this:

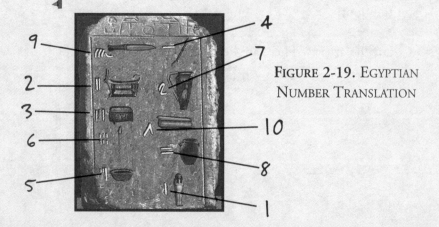

FIGURE 2-19. EGYPTIAN
NUMBER TRANSLATION

Now that you've deciphered Egyptian numerals, exit the north storeroom and go straight across the *Main Hall* to the Temple's other side room.

Temple: South Storeroom

▲ Go to the chest you can see through the doorway.

▲ Open the chest.

▲ Click on each scroll and read the exhortations to the gods.

These scrolls reveal the names of Egyptian deities and explain the significance of their symbols. You don't necessarily need these scrolls to solve any puzzles, but it's nice to know the names of the gods. (Figure 2-20 displays all the deity scrolls for easy reference.)

FIGURE 2-20. DEITY SCROLLS

▲ Approach the statue of the Egyptian warrior.

▲ Click on the warrior's skirt to open the secret compartment.

▲ Click on the scroll to open it.

FIGURE 2-21. GIVE HIM A WEDGIE WHILE YOU'RE AT IT.
HAVEN'T YOU ALWAYS WANTED TO PULL UP SOME GUY'S SKIRT
AND GRAB HIS SCROLL?

The warrior's scroll contains critical information. What kind, you ask? Hey, I'm not going to tell you. Not yet, anyway.

▲ Before you leave, you probably want to open that sarcophagus in the corner. Rats!

▲ Exit the Temple and go around to the back of the building. (If you see a cat, follow it.)

Avenue of the Obelisks

▲ Step forward to the first pair of obelisks. A voice intones, "There is meaning to all things. Even the stones speak of it." Hmmm.

▲ Approach one of the obelisks. Take careful note of the following:

    1. The glowing Egyptian numeral associated with each god. You know how to translate them now (see Figure 2-19).

    2. The background color behind each deity symbol.

▲ Examine each of the eight obelisks, noting the number and background color associated with each god.

Check out all eight obelisks, figures 22A through 22H. Because this isn't a full-color book, I describe the background colors for each deity (remember, colors can vary from one monitor to the next). First, here are the four obelisks on the left side of the avenue as you move away from the Temple:

FIGURE 2-22A. THOTH, 1, LAVENDER   FIGURE 2-22B. SET, 8, RED   FIGURE 2-22C. OSIRIS, 7, DARK GREEN   FIGURE 2-22D. BASTET, 9, BLUE

Here are the four obelisks on the right side of the avenue as you move away from the Temple:

FIGURE 2-22E. SEBEK, 4, LIGHT GREEN

FIGURE 2-22F. KNUMM, 5, PURPLE

FIGURE 2-22G. HORUS, 3, YELLOW

FIGURE 2-22H. ANNUBIS, 10, BROWN

▲ After you examine all of the obelisks, proceed down the avenue.

▲ Go through the partially closed doorway that leads into the mountainside.

Crystal Room

Welcome to the Egyptian Crystal Room. Sounds like a cheesy hotel bar, doesn't it? After the door slides open, a voice recites a simple verse:

In the crystals you will find
Gods and values are combined.

Your immediate response: Whatever, dude. Scan the room. Looks like a bunch of statues with glowing crystals. Examine any crystal more closely. Its face displays three symbols. You can rotate them. What does it all mean? If you're feeling kind of existential right now, I don't blame you.

Let's walk step-by-step through the process for manipulating the first crystal. Once you understand the puzzle logic, you'll feel a lot better. Then you can set the other crystals with ease.

How to Set the Crystals

Before we start, note the following four things:

1. Each crystal's color corresponds to the background color on a given god's obelisk outside—that is, the god on the obelisk is the god designated by the crystal's color. Note that the obelisk outside spacially match (by position) the crystals inside the Crystal Room.

2. Each crystal's top symbol represents a specific god. You must rotate to the symbol for the god designated by the crystal's color. (See the previous note.)

3. Each crystal's middle symbol represents the number associated with that god—again, a numerical association is found on the obelisks outside. But remember what the voice said: "In the crystals you will find gods and values are combined." (We'll get to that in a moment.)

4. The crystal's bottom symbol represents the god's primary attribute. These are the "secret symbols" that flashed (one for each god-head) in the crystal ball on the pedestal back in the Temple's *Main Hall*. (Refer to Figure 2-14 to review each god's secret symbols.)

ATTENTION, IMPATIENT CHEATERS! If you seek a quick solution, jump ahead to "Setting the Crystals: Quick Solution" and view figures 2-30A to 2-30H for the final crystal settings.

FIGURE 2-23. IT'S JUST THAT SIMPLE.
ROTATE THE TOP GLYPH TO THE APPROPRIATE GOD
(THE CRYSTAL'S COLOR TELLS YOU WHICH GOD). ROTATE THE
MIDDLE GLYPH TO THAT GOD'S NUMBER, ALTERED BY THE
MATH IN THE WARRIOR SCROLL. ROTATE THE BOTTOM GLYPH
TO THAT GOD'S "SECRET SYMBOL."

Setting the First Crystal

▲ Just inside the door, turn left and approach the lavender crystal.

▲ The color corresponds (sort of) to the Thoth obelisk, so click on the top symbol until Thoth's glyph appears—the ibis-headed guy with the long beak and the big ball on his head.

▲ Say "Thoth's glyph" 10 times really fast. (Just kidding.)

Now comes the tricky part. You must set the crystal's middle symbol to the correct Egyptian number. You may recall that each god glyph on Obelisk Avenue has a glowing numeral under it. You could enter that number on the crystal … but then you'd be wrong. It's the kind of mistake where people snicker behind your back and then, when you leave the room, everybody falls down laughing. That's not good. So consider the scroll you filched from the warrior's skirt back in the Temple.

FIGURE 2-24. MATH 101. SUBTRACT NUMBERS THAT COME BEFORE A GOD'S HEAD. ADD NUMBERS THAT COME AFTER IT.

Notice how the god-head glyphs are paired with Egyptian numerals? This, in essence, is a page of math. If the numeral

comes before the god's head on the warrior's scroll, subtract that number from the god's special number—that is, the glowing number paired with the god on its obelisk. If the numeral on the scroll comes after the god's head, add that number to the god's obelisk number. It's a lot of fun. (And if you figure it all out, you can go to graduate school at Yale without taking the GRE.)

Here's a quick look at this obelisk/scroll math. Remember, the first number in the equation comes from the obelisk, while the function (addition or subtraction) and the second number come from the warrior's scroll:

Sebek: 4 - 1   Set: 8 + 2
Annubis: 10 - 2   Osiris: 7 - 1
Thoth: 1 + 1   Horus: 3 + 4
Knumm: 5 + 4   Bastet: 9 - 8

Let's get more specific and apply this theory to Thoth's crystal:

FIGURE 2-25.
THOTH'S
OBELISK

The number on Thoth's obelisk was 1, remember? Now check the warrior's scroll.

FIGURE 2-26.
THOTH'S
MATH

The number next to Thoth's head on the scroll is 1, and it comes after Thoth's head. Thus, we add 1 to 1. That would be 2, as far as I know.

FIGURE 2-27.
THOTH'S
CRYSTAL NUMBER

Rotate the middle glyph to the Egyptian numeral 2. By the way, you'll see some unfamiliar glyphs as you scroll through the numbers. Ignore them.

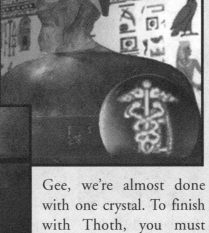

FIGURE 2-28. THOTH'S
SECRET SYMBOL

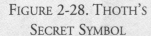

Gee, we're almost done with one crystal. To finish with Thoth, you must rotate the lavender crystal's bottom glyph to Thoth's secret symbol. Figure 2-28 displays the symbol as you found it in the crystal globe (top), and then as you entered it in Thoth's lavender crystal (bottom). Done!

Setting the Crystals: Quick Solution

Hey, only seven more crystals to go. But these will be easy, now that you know the system. Here's the quick solution to the rest of the puzzle. First, the crystals on the left side of the room, starting nearest the entry door:

FIGURE 2-29A. THOTH (LAVENDER CRYSTAL)

FIGURE 2-29B. SET (RED CRYSTAL)

FIGURE 2-29C. OSIRIS (DARK GREEN CRYSTAL)

FIGURE 2-29D. BASTET (BLUE CRYSTAL)

And here are the crystals on the right side of the room, starting nearest the entry door:

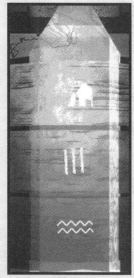

FIGURE 2-29E. SEBEK (LIGHT GREEN CRYSTAL)

FIGURE 2-29F. KNUMM (PURPLE CRYSTAL)

FIGURE 2-29G. HORUS (YELLOW CRYSTAL)

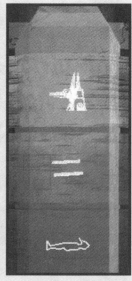

FIGURE 2-29H. ANNUBIS (BROWN CRYSTAL)

- After you set all eight crystals correctly, approach the box in the center of the room.

- Click on the tub. Watch as a red crystal forms inside the box.

- Click on the red crystal to take it. The crystal moves to the corner of the screen.

- Move forward through the open doorway.

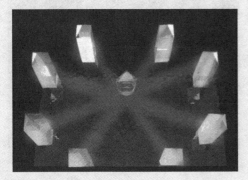

FIGURE 2-30. SNAKE ANTIDOTE. GRAB THAT RED CRYSTAL. YOU'RE GOING TO NEED IT IN A FEW SECONDS.

Cobra Hallway

As you step through the doorway, you're treated to another inspiring bit of verse:

> *There is an offering to make*
> *To appease the waiting snake.*

Apparently, these Egyptians were pretty bad poets. But it's nice of them to give advice. Fortunately, we have our "offering" now.

▲ Follow the corridor to the cobra.

▲ Drag the red crystal over the snake and release it. Easy, eh?

▲ Continue down the corridor.

FIGURE 2-31. WARM
SNAKE SPIT. IF YOU
CLICK ON THE COBRA,
YOU GET A FACEFUL OF
BLINDING VENOM.
USE THE RED CRYSTAL
ON THE SLIMY BEAST.

Pharaoh's Well: Stairway Puzzle

▲ At the end of the corridor, note the square button etched
with a stairway icon on the pillar. Look familiar? (Aha! It's
the same as the button on the power pillar back in the
Temple's *Main Hall*.)

▲ Go forward until you're looking down the well.

▲ Drag the red crystal over the water and release it.

▲ Watch the Egyptian Pharaoh spirit awaken and speak.

FIGURE 2-32. GO BACK TO SLEEP, MAN. SURE, HE'S LONG-WINDED AND POMPOUS. ALL THOSE ANCIENT GUYS WERE.

Here's a transcript of the Pharaoh spirit's message. It's a creation myth:

In the first season of all time, Ra the Creator made the good world, and all that moves and grows. He taught humankind to till the land and tame the beasts, but Ra withheld much knowledge, for He saw that we were not yet ready to receive it. We were content with gathering the fruits of the land. Our houses were made of thatch and mud, our implements of stone and clay. We built neither temple nor tomb, nor did we know the powers of medicine, or the secrets of numbers. At an appointed time, the universal God, Osiris, smiled upon us, and sent Learned Ones from a far place. They offered the gift of enlightenment to our Pharaoh and to our high-born, and promised that their offspring would be great in mind and spirit.

Clearly, you must go down the well. You can see the edge of some stairs spiraling down, but they're retracted into the wall. What now?

▲ Did you ignore my helpful tip back at the Metamorphosis God? If so, you have to go all the way back to the power pillar in the Temple *Main Hall* and click on the middle button—the one etched with a stairs icon. This powers up the stairway mechanism.

▲ Return to the pillar just before the Pharaoh's well.

▲ Click on the stairway button. If you hurry to the well, you can see the stairs extend.

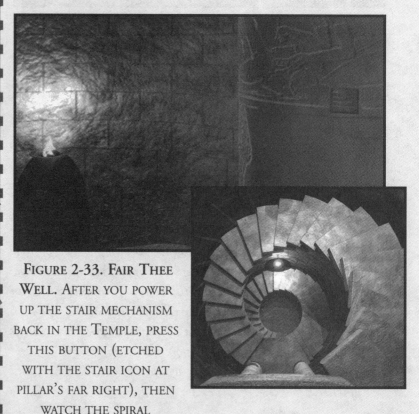

FIGURE 2-33. FAIR THEE WELL. AFTER YOU POWER UP THE STAIR MECHANISM BACK IN THE TEMPLE, PRESS THIS BUTTON (ETCHED WITH THE STAIR ICON AT PILLAR'S FAR RIGHT), THEN WATCH THE SPIRAL STAIRCASE DESCEND.

▲ Back up a step (if you're looking in the well) and turn right.

▲ Head down the stairway.

On the third forward move, a creature appears and hisses, "Trespasser!" This is the Guardian. He's not a pleasant guy. You'll get to know him better as you move along. For now, let's just continue as if nothing happened.

FIGURE 2-34. GUARDIAN. DID YOU SEE THAT? WHO WAS THAT GUY? I DON'T LIKE HIS TONE OF VOICE.

▲ After the Guardian disappears, take two more steps down the stairs.

▲ Turn right and enter the passage on the second landing.

Second Landing: The "Snakes & Gems" Game

▲ Continue forward to the room at the end of the passage.

▲ Enter the room and go forward to the pedestal.

▲ Click on the pedestal bust to awaken yet another Egyptian spirit. He says, "You want few mistakes when you play among snakes;" then snakes come out of his eyes. Those Egyptian spirits. What a fun bunch!

▲ When the animation stops, turn right and click on the wall tablet.

▲ Read the rules of the game.

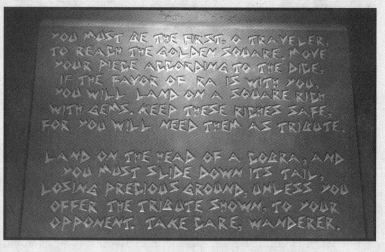

YOU MUST BE THE FIRST, O TRAVELER, TO REACH THE GOLDEN SQUARE. MOVE YOUR PIECE ACCORDING TO THE DICE; IF THE FAVOR OF RA IS WITH YOU, YOU WILL LAND ON A SQUARE RICH WITH GEMS. KEEP THESE RICHES SAFE, FOR YOU WILL NEED THEM AS TRIBUTE.

LAND ON THE HEAD OF A COBRA, AND YOU MUST SLIDE DOWN ITS TAIL, LOSING PRECIOUS GROUND, UNLESS YOU OFFER THE TRIBUTE SHOWN, TO YOUR OPPONENT. TAKE CARE, WANDERER.

FIGURE 2-35. RULES FOR "SNAKES & GEMS"

"Snakes & Gems" couldn't be simpler. It requires very little strategy, and it's pretty easy to win. To play the game:

1. Click on the pyramid-shaped die at the bottom of the screen. Your game piece moves automatically.

2. Keep clicking on the die.

3. Click more.

4. Don't stop clicking.

5. If you land on a snake block, quickly move the number of gems indicated on the front of it (I, II, or III) from your gem collection (if you have enough) to your opponent's gem collection. Don't dally. The snakes are impatient.

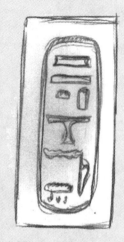

FIGURE 2-36. "SNAKES & GEMS." AN EARLY EGYPTIAN VERSION OF "CHUTES & LADDERS," WITH A NICE PAYOLA ANGLE. THIS GAME IS A DIRECT ADAPTATION OF AN ACTUAL EGYPTIAN GAME.

▲ Once you win, take the Wadjet key (the eye thing) hanging on the back wall.

▲ Back away from the game and go to the Golden Closet across the room.

▲ Put the Wadjet key in place on the right-hand closet door (over the two holes).

▲ Open the closet door and step forward.

▲ Click on the object in the marble pedestal for a close-up. The Gene Pod! (If you don't know what that is—well, you haven't been reading the professor's journal, have you?)

▲ Click on the Gene Pod to activate a message.

FIGURE 2-37. GENE POD. COOL! WHAT IS IT? CLICK ON THE POD AND THE NICE LADY WILL TELL YOU.

When you click on the Gene Pod, a queen-like person appears and speaks. Here's what she says:

Hear our thoughts. You have within your grasp a power from beyond the stars. It is the gift of enlightenment. An elevation of mind and spirit to a new and wondrous plain. The gift will not be manifest in you, but in your children and through generations to the end of time. Your descendants shall come to know new truths and devise ways to harness the unseen forces of this world. Accept this gift, and all that has been promised shall come to pass.

▲ Click on the open scroll in the closet for a close-up.

What is this thing? Remember the lawn jockey guy by the Pyramid—"Where find the scarab, you will find the key"? The Gene Pod is a scarab, so this scroll must be a key. But to what? The Pyramid on the scroll is a dead giveaway (no pun intended). The "key" is the combination to that 4-glyph tumbler lock on the door inside the Pyramid.

▲ Add up the number of items in each column—3, 10, 9, 4.

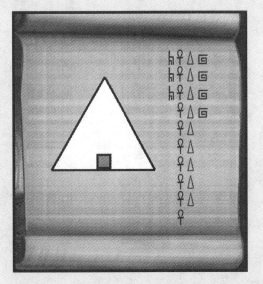

FIGURE 2-38. ONE PYRAMID COMBO, TO GO. ADD THE NUMBER OF ITEMS IN EACH COLUMN TO GET THE TUMBLER LOCK COMBINATION.

Of course, you have to translate the four-number code (3, 10, 9, 4) into Egyptian numerals. But that's easy enough now, isn't it? One other thing, though, before you go sprinting wildly back to the Pyramid. The door-unlocking mechanism in the Pyramid won't work unless you power it up first.

▲ Travel back to the Temple *Main Hall*.

Dock Temple: *Main Hall*

▲ Go to the power pillar.

▲ Click on the top (Pyramid) button.

▲ Travel across the river to the Pyramid.

Pyramid: Tumbler Lock Puzzle

▲ Move forward until you get a close-up of the tumbler lock on the door.

▲ From left to right, set the tumblers to the four-number code—3, 10, 9, 4. Of course, the tumbler numbers are Egyptian. For the code translation to Egyptian numerals, see Figure 2-39.

FIGURE 2-39. OPEN SESAME. HERE'S THE CORRECT DOOR
COMBINATION.

Setting the combination can be a bit tricky. Even I, Game
Guru, didn't get it quite right the first time. So if the door
doesn't open right away, try messing with the dials a bit.

▲ Click on the small triangle button just to the left of the
tumblers.

▲ After the door opens, enter the next room.

Pyramid: Transportal Chamber

▲ Approach the sarcophagus at the far end of the room.

▲ Continue forward. The sarcophagus lid opens automatically.

▲ Approach the transportal device (the orb).

FIGURE 2-40. TIME PASSAGE. WALK RIGHT THROUGH THIS
SARCOPHAGUS INTO THE TRANSPORTAL CHAMBER.

Watch Professor Nichols burble another message. He's ecstatic
about his discoveries, and he crows a bit about all the people
who scoffed at him in the past. Here's a transcript:

> *I can only hope you've found one of the secret artifacts. They
> are well-protected, believe me. And they are the key to our
> freedom, and the proof I need. I had them in my grasp! And
> now they've vanished. I found one in each ancient world I
> explored. If possible, you must acquire all three. Use my jour-
> nal, it will help. Without them, I'll never leave this place.
> And neither will you!*

If you wait a few seconds, a second message appears:

> *I can't wait to confront my arrogant critics. You should have
> heard what they called me—addled, misguided, scientifically
> bereft. And far worse, I can tell you. But not any more. Hard
> evidence of these discoveries will rock the scientific world! I*

can't wait to bring the artifacts back to our own time! We could end disease, hunger, avarice, and war in our own lifetime. Oh yes, yes, it's true! They hold the secrets to incredible power. I have much to tell you when we meet. They'll shower me with honors now. Shower us, I should say. The world will be ours, my friend.

Time to move on to the next Timelapse world:

▲ Click on the second button from the right—the one decorated with a green lizard. You'll see a spinning animation of a Mayan city in the orb.

▲ Click on the orb to travel to the Mayan location.

FIGURE 3-53. MAYAN FLYBY. TIME FOR MORE TIME-HOPPING.

My best shot at a map
of Mayan complex

Ocean

Castillo

Skull Temple

Jungle

Monkey
Temple

Lizard Temple

Jaguar Temple

Sun Temple

Arrival

Castillo Pyramid

Monkey Temple

Skull Temple

Jaguar Temple

CHAPTER 3
Maya

THE MAYAN COMPLEX of *Timelapse* sprawls over the jungles and cliffs of a peninsula jutting into the Caribbean Sea. The site consists of four temples surrounding a central plaza; an underground passage and pool; some wild, overgrown jungle pathways, and two more temples hidden in the dense rain forest. As in the other *Timelapse* worlds, puzzle solutions require keen observation of local objects and sounds.

FIGURE 3-1. JOURNAL MAP. HERE'S THE BASIC LAYOUT OF THE MAYAN WORLD, COURTESY OF DR. NICHOLS' JOURNAL.

Arrival: Beach Landing

As you pop out of the time gate, brushing tendrils of time off your sleeves, you find yourself on a spectacular white-sand beach. At your feet, gentle Caribbean waters lap onto the shore of the Yucatan Peninsula. All you need now is a fruity rum drink. Unfortunately, they didn't make those little cocktail umbrellas in 1135.

FIGURE 4-2. MAYAN ARRIVAL. THE MAYAN HIGH PRIESTS MUST HAVE CHERISHED THE SERENITY OF THIS BEAUTIFUL BEACH (WHEN THEY WEREN'T HACKING THROUGH THE BREASTBONES OF THEIR SACRIFICIAL VICTIMS).

▲ Turn left. The Guardian makes another of his charming appearances. Somebody please help this guy locate a life.

▲ Turn left again and climb the rocky path.

▲ At the top of the path, examine the two stelae.

Six of these stelae line the path up from the beach. Some will be important later; I'll include screen shots where appropriate. For now, just note that each stele displays a few glyphs and a central symbol on a raised square—insect, skull, jaguar, monkey, lizard, snake.

▲ At the first corner in the path, turn back toward the beach and approach the stone lizard head.

▲ Click on the lizard head to open its jaw.

▲ Take the golden amulet from its mouth.

Figure 3-3. Pair of Lizard Brains. The Guardian's taunts seem toothless, but that reptile has teeth to spare. Pluck the golden amulet from its tongue and continue up the path.

- ▲ Continue up the path, noting the stelae along the way.

- ▲ Climb the stairs to the top of the first Pyramid.

Castillo Pyramid: Chameleon Guardian

The professor's journal notes that this first pyramid bears a great resemblance to the Castillo, a sacred pyramid that dominates the great Mayan city of Chichen Itza. He calls this one "Castillo," too, and we'll do the same.

- ▲ Move forward to the pulsing electrical light on the pond platform.

- ▲ Place the golden amulet on the pulsing light. The amulet changes into a magic chameleon.

This chameleon is a tad bigger than average, and many magnitudes nastier. In fact, it is the temple guardian and won't let you pass. You must solve a puzzle first. How unique! Before you activate the puzzle, do a few quick memory calisthenics, or grab a piece of paper and a pencil. This puzzle regenerates randomly, so I can't give you a universal solution.

FIGURE 3-4. MONDO CHAMELEON. TOUCH HIM TO TRIGGER MANY SHADES OF MENACE. REPEAT THE COLOR SEQUENCE BY PUSHING THE CORRESPONDING COLORED TILES.

▲ Click on the chameleon. The lizard cycles through four colors. Memorize or jot down their order.

▲ Press the colored tiles in the order of the chameleon's color cycle.

▲ If you enter the correct color combination, the chameleon immediately cycles through five more colors.

▲ Again, press the colored tiles in the order of the chameleon's color cycle.

▲ If you enter the correct code, the persistent chameleon cycles through six more colors.

▲ Enter the six-color combination. If you do it correctly, the chameleon melts away.

▲ Proceed forward into the Pyramid.

Note
The chameleon's color cycles are generated randomly, so there is no universal solution.

At this point, you could explore the Castillo Pyramid, then exit its far door and check out the other structures around the central plaza. You'd learn that each of the three temples has a dominant motif—monkey, jaguar, and skull. You'd also learn that they're locked, so you'd better focus your attention on the Castillo Pyramid for now.

FIGURE 3-5. SURELY, TEMPLES! LOOK, THERE'S A MONKEY TEMPLE (LEFT), A JAGUAR TEMPLE (CENTER), AND A SKULL TEMPLE (RIGHT). YOU CAN ONLY ACCESS THE CASTILLO PYRAMID BEHIND YOU AT THIS POINT.

Castillo Pyramid: Activating the Metamorphosis God

Inside the Castillo Pyramid, you find a lot of interesting items, including a "god head" sculpture with a crystal globe similar to the Metamorphosis God back in Egypt. But it doesn't seem to be active yet. You must find its power source.

▲ Just inside the door, turn right and approach the 3-by-4 grid of stone tiles.

The dot-and-dash symbols on the tiles are Mayan numbers, of course. Each dash is a 5 and each dot is a 1. How do you know this? Check out the journal entry in Figure 3-6.

Journal Entry 11
There is a huge mural calendar here, and counting symbols carved on the wall.

In contrast with their sophisticated written language, the Maya used only three characters to represent numbers. A shell, a dot, and a bar.

They understood the concept zero, and used it in their calculations, a feat matched by only the Hindus and Babylonians. Could their mathematical sophistication have led to their precise calendar?

FIGURE 3-6. CRACK THE CODE. THIS PAGE FROM THE PROFESSOR'S JOURNAL SHOULD CLEAR UP SOME OF THE MYSTERY SURROUNDING THOSE DOTS AND DASHES ON THE STONE TILES.

OK, so those tiles are Mayan numbers. But what do they mean? Actually, this tile grid is a page of simple math addition. Add each number in the top horizontal row to a number in the middle horizontal row to get a sum in the bottom horizontal row. For example:

▲ Click on the tile with the Mayan symbol for the number 13 in the top row.

▲ Click on the tile with the Mayan symbol for the number 8 in the middle row.

▲ Click on the tile with the Mayan symbol for the number 21 in the bottom row.

Continue this process until you've highlighted the entire grid. Only one combination of four sums works:

Top Row	+	Middle Row	=	Bottom Row
13	+	8	=	21
14	+	9	=	23
12	+	1	=	13
20	+	2	=	22

For those who don't like mathematical grunt work, here's a no-brainer solution: Just click on the stone tiles in the order shown in Figure 3-7.

FIGURE 3-7. STONE TILES SOLUTION

After you click on the tiles in the correct order, a secret compartment opens to the left of the grid. Inside the compartment, you find a lever.

▲ Pull the lever. This opens a skylight that shines on the Metamorphosis God bust.

▲ Turn left and approach the bust.

▲ Roll the crystal globe from glyph to glyph and note how the god head morphs in relation to each.

FIGURE 3-8. METAMORPHOSIS GOD, MAYAN EDITION. CRYSTAL GLOBE, FIVE GOD HEADS—YOU SAW SOMETHING LIKE THIS BACK IN EGYPT, DIDN'T YOU?

As you roll the crystal globe from glyph to glyph, the god head transforms from god to god … but something else is happening, too. Remember the stelae on the path up from the beach? Some were marked with animal symbols similar to those on the base of the Metamorphosis God—Skull, Monkey, Jaguar, Lizard. When you roll the crystal globe in front of an animal symbol (thus transforming the god head into that animal), you also activate the stele with the corresponding animal symbol back on the beach path. Then what? Read on.

Unlocking the Temples: Calendar Wheel Puzzle

▲ Roll the crystal globe until the god head transforms into a skull—the second position from the left.

▲ Exit the Pyramid and head down the beach path.

▲ Find the stele with the skull symbol. It's at the bottom of the beach path. (See Figure 3-9.)

▲ Press the skull button—it's glowing now!—on the stele. Three of the other glyphs light up, too. We'll call these three the Skull Stele Glyphs.

FIGURE 3-9. SKULL GOD AND STELE. ROLL THE GLOBE TO THE SKULL GOD TO ACTIVATE THE SKULL STELE ON THE BEACH PATH. THEN GO TO THE SKULL STELE, CLICK ON THE GLOWING SKULL TILE, AND PAY CLOSE ATTENTION TO THE THREE GLYPHS THAT LIGHT UP.

▲ Carefully note the three Skull Stele Glyphs and return to the Castillo Pyramid.

▲ Go to the stone tile grid and turn right to face the Mayan calendar wheels.

Note that there are actually three dials—two in the left wheel and one in the right wheel. Note also that you find the three glyphs from the Skull stele on the dials, one on each dial.

▲ Turn the dials on the Mayan calendar until the three Skull Stele Glyphs (see Figure 3-9) line up across the middle.

That last step is a joke. It's not quite so simple, is it? Trying to align the three Skull Stele Glyphs on the Mayan calendar would make anyone toss up their hands and buy a strategy guide. If you turn one dial, at least one of the other dials turns as well. It can be maddening if you don't have a foolproof system. Fortunately, there is such a system. But first, let's review the interplay between the three calendar dials.

When you turn the left dial, the middle dial rotates with it in the same direction, while the right dial remains stationary.

When you turn the middle dial, both of the other dials rotate—the left dial in the same direction, the right dial in the opposite direction. However, because the two openings (where the glyphs appear) are on opposite sides of their respective wheels, all the dials appear to turn in the same direction; for example, if you pull the middle dial down, the other two dials move down. But the middle and left dials turn clockwise, while the right dial actually turns counter-clockwise.

When you turn the right dial, the left dial rotates in the same direction, and the middle dial remains stationary. Again, the placement of the wheel openings creates the illusion that the left and right dials are turning in opposite directions. If you pull the right dial up, the left dial moves down. But both dials actually rotate in the same clockwise direction.

FIGURE 3-10. MAYAN CALENDAR WHEELS

Now that we've got this Mayan calendar dial movement straight, here's a surefire method for aligning your three glyphs.

How to Set the Mayan Calendar: The 4-Step Method

1. Turn the middle dial until the correct glyph on that dial lines up in the center position.

2. Turn the right dial until the correct glyph on the left dial (always a Mayan number) lines up in the center position. (Remember, the middle dial doesn't move when you turn the right dial, so your first glyph stays in position.)

3. Carefully counting your moves, move the middle dial down until the correct glyph on the right dial lines up in the center position.

4. Did you count your moves in the last step? I hope so. Move the left dial up the same number of moves. Bingo. You're done.

FIGURE 3-11. SKULL CALENDAR SETTING.

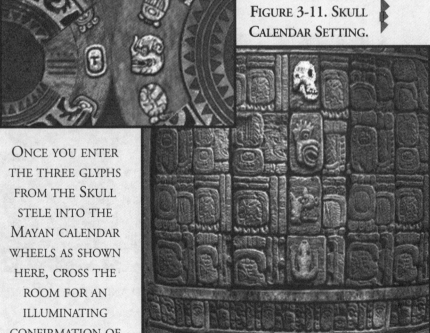

ONCE YOU ENTER THE THREE GLYPHS FROM THE SKULL STELE INTO THE MAYAN CALENDAR WHEELS AS SHOWN HERE, CROSS THE ROOM FOR AN ILLUMINATING CONFIRMATION OF YOUR SUCCESS.

When you align the Skull Stele Glyphs correctly on the Mayan calendar wheels, an audio reward confirms your success. Congratulations! You just unlocked the Skull Temple out in the central plaza.

▲ From the Mayan calendar, go right, forward, right, forward twice, and turn right to face the crystal skull.

▲ Step forward twice to the skull, then turn right to see the wall carving. The Skull Glyph on the carving glows, confirming that you've completed the Skull portion of the calendar puzzle.

Before you run off to explore the Skull Temple, save time by unlocking the three other Mayan temples first—Monkey, Jaguar, and Lizard. The method for each is the same as for the Skull Temple, so I'll walk you quickly through the following steps.

Return to the Metamorphosis God and roll the globe to the monkey head. This activates the Monkey stele down on the beach path. Go to the Monkey stele, push the glowing monkey tile, and note the three glyphs that light up.

FIGURE 3-12. MONKEY GOD AND STELE

FIGURE 3-13. MONKEY CALENDAR SETTING

Go to the Mayan calendar wheels and use the foregoing four-step method to align the three Monkey Stele Glyphs. Aligning the glyphs correctly unlocks the Monkey Temple.

FIGURE 3-14. JAGUAR GOD AND STELE

Return to the Metamorphosis God and roll the globe to the jaguar head. This activates the Jaguar stele down on the beach path. Go to the Jaguar stele, push the glowing jaguar tile, and note the three glyphs that light up.

FIGURE 3-15. JAGUAR CALENDAR SETTING

Go to the Mayan calendar wheels and use the foregoing four-step method to align the three Jaguar Stele Glyphs. Aligning the glyphs correctly unlocks the Jaguar Temple.

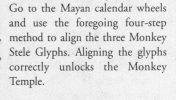

Return to the Metamorphosis God and roll the globe to the lizard head. This activates the Lizard stele down on the beach path. Go to the Lizard stele, push the glowing lizard tile, and note the three glyphs that light up.

FIGURE 3-16. LIZARD GOD AND STELE

Go to the Mayan calendar wheels and use the foregoing four-step method to align the three Lizard Stele Glyphs. Aligning the glyphs correctly unlocks the Lizard Temple.

FIGURE 3-17. LIZARD CALENDAR SETTING

Note
By the way, you probably haven't seen the Lizard Temple yet. It's out in the jungle.

When you've correctly aligned each set of stele glyphs on the Mayan calendar, all four "confirmation glyphs" on the wall carving next to the crystal skull will glow (as in Figure 3-18). If any of these confirmation glyphs do not glow, then you didn't properly set the Mayan calendar dials corresponding to that glyph. Take two aspirin and try again.

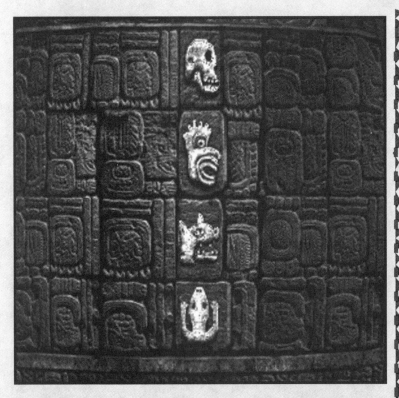

FIGURE 3-18. YOU'VE GOT THAT SPECIAL GLOW. AND NOW, YOUR WORK IN THE CASTILLO PYRAMID IS DONE.

Now you're ready to explore the other structures in the Mayan complex. Start with the three temples surrounding the central plaza.

▲ Exit the Castillo Pyramid through its far door.

▲ Descend the stairs to the plaza.

▲ Enter the temple on the right.

Skull Temple: Skeleton Construction Kit

This place is kind of grisly. Blood-washed walls, etc. Those Mayan priests were certainly a fascinating bunch of homicidal maniacs. An examination of the Skull Temple might induce some pretty interesting nightmares.

FIGURE 3-19. THE SKULL TEMPLE

Note
To enter the Skull Temple, you must have unlocked it by setting the Mayan calendar wheels correctly back in the Castillo Pyramid. If you haven't done so, refer to the previous section, "Unlocking the Temples," for directions.

▲ Enter the Skull Temple.

▲ Inside the door, turn right to face the partial skeleton hanging on the wall.

▲ Reassemble the skeleton from the bone pile on the floor.

You must place 13 of these bones on the skeleton; a few useless extra bones litter the pile as well. Use this bone-by-bone construction guide:

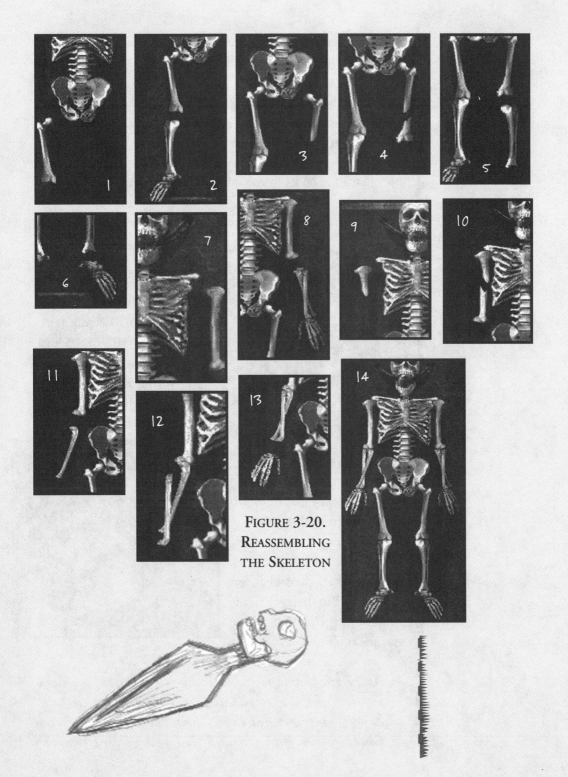

FIGURE 3-20.
REASSEMBLING
THE SKELETON

- ▲ Once you've reassembled the skeleton, click on its skull to open the jaw.

- ▲ Take the jewel from the skeleton's mouth.

- ▲ Turn around to face the skull disk on the opposite wall.

- ▲ Place the jewel in the hole in the center of the skull disk.

- ▲ Watch the message from the Mayan priest.

FIGURE 3-21. MAYAN MYTHOLOGY 101. AFTER YOU PLACE THE JEWEL IN THE CENTER OF THE SKULL DISK, A MAYAN PRIEST APPEARS WITH AN INTERESTING TALE TO TELL.

When the Mayan priest finishes speaking, the message portal closes. You can view the message again—just click on the portal, then click on the jewel. But here's a transcript of the priest's tale of the Mayan "migration":

As the priests did prophisize, Itzam-Na appeared as a blinding light atop our temples, and was seen in all our city-states at once. He summoned us to climb to the light, and be transported to our blissful reward. But many feared that they

would be sacrificed upon the high altars, and fled and hid among the jungle vines. Our learned brethren knew not this fear, and so climbed the steps, and saw that the steps did not end, but became a stairway to the heavens. So did our civilization cease to be a united people, and in the cycle of time the jungle shroud grew to cloak our once mighty cities.

FIGURE 3-22. WHAT ARE THESE GUYS DOING? AFTER THE MAYAN PRIEST'S MESSAGE, THIS ODD ICON OF TWO FIGURES APPEARS ON THE MESSAGE PORTAL.

▲ After the message, carefully note the icon that appears in the message portal. (See Figure 3-22.) This will be very important later.

▲ Exit the Skull Temple.

▲ Go directly across the plaza to the Monkey Temple.

Monkey Temple: Spider Maze

Welcome to the Monkey House. There's a lot of good monkey stuff in here, which is great if you're into monkeys. If not, we have spiders. Spiders always make good puzzle-related items.

FIGURE 3-23. THE MONKEY TEMPLE

Note

To enter the Monkey Temple, you must have unlocked it by setting the Mayan calendar wheels correctly back in the Castillo Pyramid. If you haven't done so, refer to the section "Unlocking the Temples" for directions.

▲ Enter the temple and move forward to the monkey god head.

▲ Click on the head for this advice: "Defeat the darkness to reveal the light." What's it mean? I'm not sure. But it sounds logical, doesn't it?

▲ Back away from the monkey god, turn left, and approach the shriveled monkey head on the stick.

FIGURE 3-24. SHRIVELED MONKEY ON A STICK. MMM, ONE OF MY FAVORITE CARNIVAL TREATS. TOUCH THE MONKEY. GO AHEAD. TOUCH IT!

▲ Touch the shriveled monkey head. It comes alive, briefly. This also activates the maze to your left.

▲ Turn left and approach the maze.

As you approach, the monkey head inside the maze opens its mouth and a green spider crawls out. This spider is your guy. Those five red spiders patrolling the maze are the bad guys. Your goal is to work your green spider down to the jewel at the bottom of the maze while avoiding the red spiders, who will eat your spider if they encounter him. Note the following:

1. The maze is divided into four sectors.

2. You must guide your spider to the hole at the far end of each sector.

3. Single red spiders patrol each of the first three sectors; two red spiders patrol the final sector.

4. Each red spider patrols in a prescribed, unalterable pattern.

Tip

Observe the red spider(s) in your current sector before you make your move. Enemy spiders patrol in a very predictable pattern. Once you figure out the pattern, it's fairly easy to sneak past. Also note the "snake" shortcuts. To use one, click on the snake's tail and guide your green spider into the tail; your spider emerges from the snake's mouth.

FIGURE 3-25. THE SPIDER MAZE. GUIDE YOUR GREEN SPIDER PAST THE EVIL RED SPIDERS DOWN TO THE JEWEL AT THE BOTTOM. THEN PUSH OUT THE JEWEL.

▲ Once your spider reaches the jewel, move the spider just above the jewel, then click below the jewel. Your spider pushes it out. The jewel automatically moves to your inventory.

▲ Back away from the maze, turn left, and approach the monkey disk.

▲ Place the jewel in the hole in the center of the disk.

▲ Watch the message from another Mayan priest.

FIGURE 3-26. YET ANOTHER MAYAN MESSAGE.

THIS PRIEST SPEAKS OF MAYAN CULTURE AT ITS HIGH POINT ... AND THE APPROACHING END FORETOLD BY ITS PROPHETS.

Here's a transcript of the priest's message:

For many generations our civilization flourished, and our kings ruled the lands. Sky-watchers studied the heavens, and could foretell the cycles of the stars, and the fortunes of men.

So also did our priests measure time and record all days and years that passed. And they saw the cycle of our people was nearing its end, and foretold the return of our great god Itzam-Na.

FIGURE 3-27. ODD COUPLE. ANOTHER PAIR OF MAYAN FIGURES IS ETCHED ON THIS MESSAGE PORTAL. GATHER THE WHOLE SET! TRADE WITH FRIENDS!

▲ After the message, carefully note the icon of the figures that appears in the message portal. (See Figure 3-27.) You'll need it later.

▲ Exit the Monkey Temple into the plaza.

▲ At the center of the plaza, turn left and go toward the Jaguar Temple.

▲ At the bottom of the Jaguar Temple stairs, an open entry leads down into a dark underground passage. Don't enter it yet. Instead, turn right, take a step forward, turn left, and climb the stairs to the temple door.

Jaguar Temple

OK, so that bloody handprint by the entry door doesn't look good. Plus, jaguars are vicious carnivores. That doesn't bode well either. The professor's journal mentions that the jaguar is a Mayan symbol of power, and its mark is everywhere in the complex. But here, in the Jaguar Temple, lies the heart of the jaguar cult.

FIGURE 3-28. THE JAGUAR TEMPLE

Note

To enter the Jaguar Temple, you must have unlocked it by setting the Mayan calendar wheels correctly back in the Castillo Pyramid. If you haven't done so, refer to the section "Unlocking the Temples" for directions.

▲ Enter the Jaguar Temple and turn right.

▲ Go forward until you get a close-up of the stone box.

This is a lockbox. Your job is to deduce the four-glyph combination that unlocks it. Four quadrants divide the front of the box—one glyph per quadrant. The quadrants correspond to the four compass points—north, south, east, west. If you click on a glyph, it mutates—the background color changes, or the glyph inverts, or the shape itself changes. If you

cycle through all the changes, you find four glyph shapes and six versions of each shape, for a total of 24 glyph combinations for each quadrant. Each quadrant cycles through the same 24-glyph combination.

▲ Take one step back and examine the jaguar mural on the wall.

FIGURE 3-29. WALL JAG. THAT BEAST LOOKS FORMIDABLE. THE FOUR GLYPHS AROUND HIM INDICATE WHAT TO ENTER IN THE LOCKBOX.

Note the four glyphs around the jaguar mural, one at each of the four compass points. These indicate the correct glyph shapes for the quadrants of the lockbox. But they do not indicate the correct background colors. You must go elsewhere to find that information.

▲ Back away from the jaguar mural and turn left to face the skull pile.

▲ Take a step toward the skulls and turn left to the reclining figure. See that dial above him?

▲ Step forward for a close-up of the dial.

FIGURE 3-30. COLOR COMPASS. THIS DIAL INDICATES THE CORRECT BACKGROUND COLORS FOR THE FOUR GLYPH POSITIONS ON THE LOCKBOX. NORTH IS WHITE, SOUTH BLACK, EAST YELLOW, AND WEST RED.

Aha! Four color-coded quadrants corresponding to the compass points. These are the correct background colors for the four quadrants of the lockbox combination.

▲ Return to the lockbox.

▲ Enter the correct combination, using the mural glyphs and the background colors from the dial. (See Figure 3-31.)

▲ When the box opens, take the golden jaguar head.

FIGURE 3-31. LOCKBOX COMBO. HERE'S THE CORRECT FOUR-GLYPH COMBINATION FOR THE LOCKBOX. SINCE THIS ISN'T A FULL-COLOR STRATEGY GUIDE, I'LL NAME THE BACKGROUND COLORS—NORTH IS WHITE, SOUTH IS BLACK, EAST IS YELLOW, AND WEST IS THE DARKER OF THE TWO REDS IN THE COLOR CYCLE.

Note

Note that there are two "reddish" colors in the glyph background color cycle. The glyph in the west quadrant requires the darker of the two reds in the cycle. Note the correct shape of the west glyph as well—with the correct red background, the glyph's three dots are on the bottom.

▲ Back up two steps from the lockbox and turn left to face the skull pile again.

▲ Go forward to the skulls, then left one step to the crucible over the fire.

▲ Place the golden jaguar head in the crucible and wait until it melts.

▲ After the head melts and pours out of the crucible, click on the stone cup to dump blood on the red-hot heart mold. This cools the mold, although it's a few seconds before you can touch it.

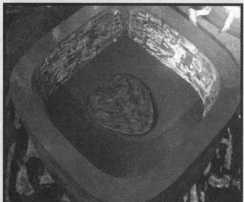

FIGURE 3-32. BLOODY HEAD SMELTING. BOY, IS THIS FUN! MELT THE HEAD INTO A HEART MOLD, POUR BLOOD TO COOL IT. THOSE MAYANS HAD ALL THE GOOD JOBS.

▲ Take out the molded heart.

▲ Go across the room to the reclining figure holding a cup.

▲ Put the heart in the cup. The heart transforms into a jewel.

▲ Take the jewel.

▲ Turn right, go forward, then turn right again to face the jaguar disk.

▲ Place the jewel in the center of the disk.

▲ Watch the Mayan priest's message.

FIGURE 3-33. JAGUAR JEWEL. MAKE A JEWEL IN THE RECLINING FIGURE'S CUP, THEN PUT IT IN THE CENTER OF THE JAGUAR DISK. YOU'LL GET A MESSAGE AND AN IMPORTANT VISUAL CLUE.

Here's a transcript of the message:

We children of the maize were blessed with knowledge and power. A mighty empire sprang from our works, and great stairways to heaven rose within our cities. The secrets of counting were revealed to us, and all numbers became known, even to infinity. We studied the movements of the heavenly orbs, and foresaw the times when the moon would hide the sun. We turned our spoken words into symbols, that paper and stone might bear witness to our deeds. And in gratitude for all that we had been given, we gave blood sacrifices that Itzam-Na might behold the devotion of his people.

FIGURE 3-34. JAGUAR
TEMPLE CLUE.
HERE'S ANOTHER
VISUAL CLUE YOU'LL
NEED FOR THE FINAL
PUZZLE IN THE
MAYAN COMPLEX.

▲ After the message portal closes, carefully note the icon on
the disk.

▲ Exit the Jaguar Temple.

▲ Turn right at the bottom of the temple stairs, step forward, then turn right again to face the entrance to the
underground passage.

▲ Enter the passage.

FIGURE 3-35. UNDERGROUND ENTRY. THIS ENTRANCE LEADS DOWN TO THE CENOTE SACRIFICIAL POOL, A REALLY CHEERY PLACE.

Underground Passage: Crossing the Chasm

Underground passages are cool. This one leads to a jungle. If that isn't cool enough, then know that a gaping chasm blocks your way. Chasms are always interesting. This one's no exception. At the bottom lies a cenote sacrificial pool, considered by Mayans to be a gateway to the underworld.

▲ Descend the stairs and follow the bone-littered path to the chasm.

▲ Look down the chasm. Uh-oh. Who dropped the bridge?

FIGURE 3-36. LOW BRIDGE. REALLY LOW. TO PULL THE BRIDGE BACK UP, YOU MUST TAKE ON CHAC. HE'S THAT RAIN GOD OVER THERE—THE ONE HOLDING THE SKULLS. GOOD LUCK.

▲ Turn right to face Chac the Rain God.

▲ Click on Chac for a close-up. He says: "To breach the mighty chasm, the cycle of victory must repeat three times."

FIGURE 3-37. "SPIDER, SCORPION, FROG." CHAC'S GAME IS GRUESOME, BUT FUN. HERE, YOUR SCORPION SKEWERS CHAC'S FROG. YES!

How to Play "Spider, Scorpion, Frog"

Chac's challenge is a horror-movie version of "Rock, Paper, Scissors." Thus, it's a game of pure chance. You control the left side of the game board, and Chac (the computer) controls the right side. Move your cursor over the three holes—two eyes and a nose—on your skull. See how they light up red?

Here's how the game works:

1. If you click on the bottom eye-hole, a scorpion emerges.

2. If you click on the top eye-hole, a frog hops out.

3. If you click on the nose-hole, a spider crawls out.

4. After you choose your creature, Chac (the computer) responds with a random creature choice.

5. Who wins? Spider beats scorpion, scorpion stings frog, frog eats spider.

6. If your creature defeats Chac's creature, a red gemstone appears in the embossed space at the bottom of the board. If Chac's creature wins, a blue gemstone appears on his side.

7. First contestant to win three creature confrontations wins a round. A gemstone then appears in one of the three holes at the top of the board on the winner's side.

8. The contestant who wins three rounds wins the game.

9. If Chac wins the game, you start a new game. If you win the game, Chac grouses a bit and raises the bridge. (The bridge stays up for the rest of the game.)

Note
You can return and play Chac in a friendly game of "Spider, Scorpion, Frog" anytime you want.

- ▲ After you defeat Chac, back away from the game board and watch as the bridge is raised.

- ▲ Cross the bridge.

- ▲ Climb the stairs on the other side of the chasm.

Mayan Jungle: Idol Roadblock

You emerge from the underground passage into lush green jungle. You know from the professor's journal that two other Mayan structures—the Lizard Temple and the Sun Temple—lie out here somewhere, so plunge ahead into the bush.

FIGURE 3-38. POLLY WANT A CLUE? LISTEN TO WHAT THIS PARROT HAS TO SAY.

- ▲ Move forward down the passage.

- ▲ When you pass the parrot, it speaks. Clue alert!

- ▲ Continue to the fork in the path. A stone idol blocks the way, saying, "You cannot pass without a sacrifice."

FIGURE 3-39. NO IDOL THREAT. BIG BOY WANTS TO HELP YOU, BUT HE CAN'T LET YOU PASS UNTIL YOU SCROUNGE UP A PAIR OF EYES FOR HIM.

The path that runs past the stone idol is clogged by vines. The other path seems clear, but if you step forward, poisoned darts strike and blind you. Worse, the Guardian taunts you. What does the idol want? Turn to face it. The idol speaks again: "I cannot see to cleave your path." The idol wants to see. It probably needs some eyes.

▲ Turn back to the path, facing away from the idol. See the glint of light on that branch up ahead?

▲ Move forward to the branch with the orchids.

▲ Click on the biggest orchid to get the orange gem.

FIGURE 3-40. EYE OF THE FLOWER. FOLLOW THAT GLINT UNTIL YOU REACH THE ORCHID BRANCH. THEN PLUCK THE GEM FROM THE BIGGEST ORCHID.

▲ Return to the idol.

▲ Place the orange gem in the idol's eye—the eye to your right.

▲ Press in the eye with the gem.

▲ Take the machete that appears in the idol's mouth. The machete moves into position over the vines.

▲ Keep clicking on the machete until the path is clear.

▲ Before we traipse off down the cleared path, let's clear the other path too.

▲ Turn right to the spider web. Did you catch the parrot's hint earlier?

▲ A spider hunkers over a gem in the center of the web—the "heart of silk." When the spider drops, grab the gem.

FIGURE 3-41. BUNGIE JUMPER. WHEN THE SPIDER DROPS, GRAB THE GREEN GEM IN THE CENTER OF THE WEB. HURRY!

▲ Turn back to the idol.

▲ Place the green gem in the idol's empty eye.

▲ Press in the eye with the green gem. Now the path to the left is clear—no more darts.

▲ Move forward down the right path to the Lizard Temple.

Lizard Temple (Upper Level): Crystal Pyramid

The Lizard Temple has two levels. The upper level is an open courtyard featuring the usual stunning interior design elements—shimmering pool, potted plants, wall carvings and murals, and, of course, skulls. The temple's lower level is a watery catacomb that sequesters both the big items you need to complete your Mayan excursion. This level is inaccessible until you solve the upper level's diabolical Crystal Pyramid puzzle.

Note

To enter the Lizard Temple, you must have unlocked it by setting the Mayan calendar wheels correctly back in the Castillo Pyramid. If you haven't done so, refer to the section "Unlocking the Temples" for directions.

FIGURE 3-42. LIZARD TEMPLE. AH, THERE IT IS. YOU KNEW THE LIZARD TEMPLE WAS OUT HERE SOMEWHERE. THE PROFESSOR'S JOURNAL TOLD YOU SO.

▲ From the pyramid's entry door, step forward five times and turn right.

▲ Take three steps forward toward the lizard disk on the wall. (Don't go all the way to the disk.)

▲ Click on the large stone vat under the lizard disk for a close-up.

▲ Take the stone heart.

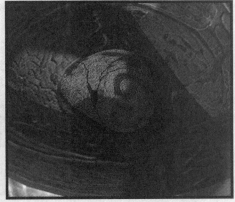

FIGURE 3-43. HAVE A HEART.
YOU'LL GET A HEARTY SURPRISE OUT
OF THAT VAT UNDER THE LIZARD
DISK ON THE WALL.

▲ After you get the stone heart, move back to see the lizard wall disk.

▲ Step forward to the lizard wall disk and turn right.

▲ Click on the piece of parchment on the floor just to the left of the potted flowering plant.

FIGURE 3-44. HAIR SAVER. PEEK AT THAT PARCHMENT ON THE FLOOR, THEN COMPARE THE FIGURES IN THE SEQUENCE TO THE NUMBERED FIGURES IN JOURNAL ENTRY 39. IF YOU DON'T, YOU'LL HAVE AN AWFULLY UNPLEASANT TIME TRYING TO SOLVE THE CRYSTAL PYRAMID PUZZLE.

The parchment contains a sequence of 22 Mayan head symbols. If you've been consulting the professor's journal, these figures might look familiar. Check Journal Entry 39. Clearly, this is a number code. A quick translation: 5, 4, 5, 5, 4, 6, 6, 5, 5, 8, 8, 5, 8, 8, 5, 5, 8, 6, 8, 4, 8, 5. But why are some figures red and some black?

▲ Turn right and move forward seven times to the circular mural on the far wall. (If you see a close-up of the rug, you've gone too far. Take one step back.)

▲ Turn right. You should see a crocodile on a podium.

▲ Place the stone heart in the bowl on the floor in front of the podium. A crystalline pyramid appears—the same one mentioned in the professor's Journal Entry 39. The crystal encases a tree.

▲ Step forward to the crystalline pyramid. A voice says, "Unbroken steps will light your way to the underworld."

FIGURE 3-45. CRYSTAL PYRAMID. MOVE THE LIZARD TO LIGHT THE TIERS OF THE PYRAMID. CAN YOU LIGHT ALL 22 TIERS IN EXACTLY 22 MOVES? NO WAY!

Wow. What does this odd apparition mean? Again, check Entry 39 in the professor's journal. The crystalline pyramid depicts the Mayan belief in a universe that consists of a central human plane with 13 tiers of heaven above and nine tiers of the dark underworld below. From the middle of the pyramid up there are seven layers—a top layer (one tier) and six more layers with two tiers apiece, one on each side. That adds up to 13 upper tiers. From the middle down there are five layers—a bottom layer (one tier) and four more layers with two tiers apiece, for a total of nine tiers. Add up all the tiers and you have 22.

And you're saying, So?

So let's discuss the puzzle. The object is to move the lizard so that it lights up all 22 tiers around the outside of the pyramid. Here's how it works:

1. See the lizard at the very top of the pyramid? He is, in effect, your "game piece"—you direct the lizard's movement around the pyramid.

2. Click on the skulls under the pyramid to move the lizard.

3. When the lizard lands on an unlit tier, that tier lights up. If the lizard lands on a lighted tier, that tier darkens. The moment this happens, you lose. Why? Because you have only 22 moves to light all 22 tiers.

4. To restart the game, just turn away from the pyramid, then turn back.

5. The three skulls on the left cause the lizard to move in a counterclockwise direction; the three skulls on the right cause the lizard to move in a clockwise direction.

6. Each skull has a Mayan number engraved on its forehead (from left to right: 4, 5, 8, 5, 6, 8). This number indicates the number of tiers the lizard climbs when you click on that skull.

7. The number of vertebrae under each skull represent the number of times you can use that skull to move the lizard. Each time you click on a skull, the spinal stack sinks one vertebra down, indicating that you've used up a turn with that skull. When the skull lowers all the way to the floor, it is spent—you can't use it anymore.

Note

Before you begin playing, count all the vertebrae in the stacks under the six skulls. There are exactly 22! This means you get 22 moves in the game to light the 22 tiers. You have no margin for error. If your lizard lands on any lighted square and darkens it, you lose the game.

Look difficult? It is, unless you're a math genius ... or unless you found the parchment (see Figure 3-44) by the lizard wall disk. I gave you the 22-number sequence from the parchment earlier. The numbers refer to the numbers etched on each of the skulls, so the sequence shows you the order to click on the skulls. The black numbers in the sequence refer to the skulls on the right side of the pyramid. The red numbers refer to the skulls on the left side of the pyramid.

To solve the Crystal Pyramid puzzle: Click on the skulls in the order listed below. The number refers to the Mayan numeral engraved on the skull's forehead; L indicates a left skull, R a right skull:

1. 5R
2. 4L
3. 5R
4. 5R
5. 4L
6. 6R
7. 6R
8. 5L
9. 5L
10. 8R
11. 8R
12. 5L
13. 8L
14. 8L
15. 5L
16. 5L
17. 8R
18. 6R
19. 8L
20. 4L
21. 8L
22. 5R

After you light up all 22 tiers, the lizard turns to gold and moves to your inventory at the corner of the screen.

▲ Back away from the puzzle, turn left, and step forward. You should see a close-up of the floor.

▲ Click on the floor (lower part of screen). A small panel appears.

▲ Place the golden lizard on the panel. The lizard disappears.

- ▲ Click on the panel to activate the stair mechanism.

- ▲ Step back to let the floor open.

- ▲ Descend the stairs to the lower level of the temple.

FIGURE 3-46. GRAND OPENING.

PUT THE GOLDEN LIZARD IN THE FLOOR PANEL TO ACTIVATE THE SECRET STAIRWAY DOWN TO THE LOWER LEVEL OF THE LIZARD TEMPLE.

Lizard Temple (Lower Level): Gene Pod Trap

- ▲ From the bottom of the stairs, head forward into the watery cavern.

- ▲ Follow the stepping stones to the left to the open pit.

- ▲ Continue forward, crossing the pit using the plank.

- ▲ Turn left. Another Gene Pod! Take it, listen to the message, then watch the podium rise.

- ▲ Grab the mallet from the open compartment.

FIGURE 3-47. MAYAN GENE POD. GRAB THAT POD TO COMPLETE YOUR COLLECTION. AND TAKE THAT MALLET, TOO. WAIT A SECOND … DID YOU HEAR A NOISE?

When you turn to go … hey, you're trapped. When you took the Gene Pod and the mallet, the podium rose up, lowering a stalactite gate from the ceiling and blocking your escape. You must pile stuff onto the podium to rebalance the weight. And it must be the exact weight—too little or too much, and the stalactite gate stays put.

FIGURE 3-48. ESCAPE POD. PILE THESE OBJECTS ONTO THE GENE POD PODIUM TO REOPEN THE STALACTITE GATE AND ESCAPE THE CHAMBER.

▲ Pile the objects shown in Figure 3-48 onto the podium.

▲ Turn left and go over the plank bridge and stepping stones to the intersection.

▲ Turn left and approach the stalactite gate.

Lizard Temple (Lower Level): Stalactite Gate

Boy, those stalactites are big. Try to bash them down with the mallet—go ahead, give it a shot. Instead of crunching destruction, you get five beautiful tones. Apparently, a musical code opens the door. The Mayans, for all their bloody ritual, prefer finesse to brute strength in their puzzle solutions.

▲ Click on the mallet indentation to the right of the stalactite gate. You hear an eight-tone melody.

▲ Repeat the eight-tone melody on the stalactites with the mallet.

Tip
Here's a quick solution for the musically impaired. From left to right, number the stalactites 1 to 5. Then play the stalactites in this order—5, 3, 4, 2, 2, 5, 5, 1.

FIGURE 3-49. MAKE MALLET MUSIC. TOUCH THAT MALLET-SHAPED INDENTATION TO HEAR A MELODY. THEN REPEAT IT ON THE STALACTITES.

▲ After you open the stalactite gate, enter the tomb chamber.

▲ Approach the open tomb.

▲ Take the jewel from the skeleton's hand. He won't give it up at first, but just keep tugging—that is, click and hold on the jewel, then jerk the mouse from side to side. The poor corpse releases the jewel eventually.

FIGURE 3-50. GRAVE BUSINESS. TAKE THE JEWEL. DON'T FEEL BAD. HE DOESN'T NEED IT ANYMORE.

▲ Go back upstairs to the upper level of the Lizard Temple.

▲ Approach the lizard disk on the far wall.

▲ Put the jewel in the center of the disk and watch the message from the Mayan priest.

Here's what the priest says this time:

Time has no beginning and no end, but is a great cycle, and so it was that in the fourth cycle of the world, a time of renewal came upon the children of the maize. The god of all knowledge, Itzam-Na, came down from his dwelling place among the stars to offer a wondrous destiny to our people. And our priests did accept this gift, and through a sting from the sacred idol, the essence of Itzam-Na flowed into their blood, and his wisdom was passed on through their seed. Thereafter did the descendants of our priests become learned in all things.

FIGURE 3-51. LIZARD TEMPLE CLUE. HERE'S THE FINAL ICON FROM THE MAYAN PRIESTS.

▲ After the message portal closes, carefully note the icon on the disk.

▲ Exit the Lizard Temple.

▲ Follow the jungle path back to the stone idol.

▲ Take the path that runs left of the idol.

▲ Follow the path to the Sun Temple.

Sun Temple: Transportal Access

The Sun Temple is the hidden heart of the Mayan complex. You can't enter this building until you find the jewels in each of the other four temples and place them in their respective temple disks.

FIGURE 3-52. THE SUN TEMPLE

▲ Climb the stairs to the Sun Temple door.

▲ Examine the disk on the door. Note that it holds all four of the jewels you found in the other temples. (If fewer than four jewels decorate the disk, you're not ready to enter this temple yet.)

Note the hole in the middle of the disk. That's right, you need one more jewel. But where could it be? It's a jungle out there.

FIGURE 3-53. SUN TEMPLE DOOR. LOOKS LIKE WE NEED ONE MORE JEWEL FOR THAT DISK.

▲ At the Sun Temple door, turn around to face the jungle.

▲ Move forward 10 times. You should end up at the base of the fallen carved head.

▲ Take the jewel: It's tucked into the palm fronds at the bottom right corner of the screen. (See Figure 3-54.)

▲ Return to the Sun Temple door.

FIGURE 3-54. PALM THAT JEWEL. THE FINAL JEWEL IS
TUCKED INTO THE PALM FRONDS AT THE BASE OF THE
FALLEN CARVED HEAD.

▲ Place the final jewel into the center hole of the disk.

▲ Move forward to enter the temple.

▲ Continue forward to the door with the slider puzzle.

Here's where you use those icon clues from the other temples.
The object of this puzzle is to move the slider tiles around until you
recreate the four disk icons from the four temples. You must assemble each icon in the specific puzzle corner indicated by the puzzle
border's bars or dots. You can't just arrange the four icons any way
you want. And I'm sorry to say that the puzzle regenerates randomly every time you approach or restart it. Thus, I can give you
no universal set of moves to solve it. You're on your own, pal.

How to Arrange the Sun Slider Puzzle

Look carefully at the puzzle's border. A red bar appears on the upper left, two blue dots on the lower left, a single orange dot on the upper right, and a green bar on the lower right. If you examine the icons from the four temples (see foregoing figures 3-22, 3-27, 3-34, and 3-51), you find the same sets of bars and dots.

1. The Jaguar icon has two blue dots, so you must assemble it in the lower left corner of the slider puzzle.

2. The Skull icon has a red bar, so you must assemble it in the upper left corner of the slider puzzle.

3. The Monkey icon has one orange dot, so you must assemble it in the upper right corner of the slider puzzle.

4. The Lizard icon has a green bar, so you must assemble it in the lower right corner of the slider puzzle.

Note
When you assemble an icon in its proper position in the puzzle, the pieces fuse.

FIGURE 3-55.
SOLUTION TO SLIDER
PUZZLE

▲ After you solve the slider puzzle, move forward to enter the transportal chamber.

▲ Proceed to the orb and listen to Professor Nichols speak again.

▲ Click on the second button from the left—the one illustrated with a flying insect. You'll see a spinning animation of ancient Anasazi dwellings in the orb.

▲ Click on the orb to travel to the Anasazi site.

FIGURE 3-56. NEXT STOP, ANASAZI-VILLE. CLICK ON THE
SECOND BUTTON FROM THE LEFT TO DIVE
A THOUSAND YEARS OR SO DOWN THE TIME TUNNEL TO YOUR
NEXT DESTINATION—THE ANCIENT ANASAZI OF THE
AMERICAN SOUTHWEST.

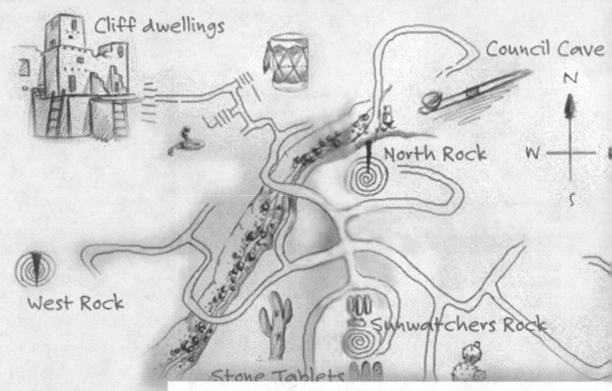

Cliff dwellings

Council Cave

North Rock

N

W · S

West Rock

Sunwatchers Rock

Stone Tablets

My landing

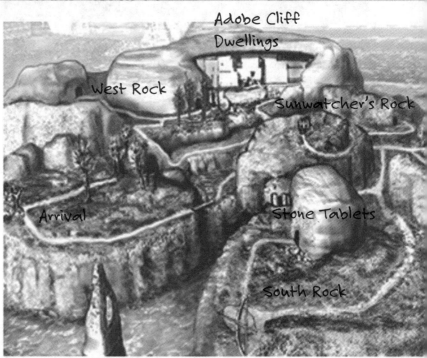

Adobe Cliff
Dwellings

West Rock

Sunwatcher's Rock

Arrival

Stone Tablets

South Rock

CHAPTER 4
Anasazi

East Rock

THE ANASAZI WORLD of *Timelapse* is a peaceful, tranquil desert. The professor describes it well in his journal: "Even the colors here are soothing, the landscape a palette of muted pastel shades, gray boulders rising from a dune sea of sand, russet cliffs layered with streaks of millennia. Rock formations tower over the parched ground and above it all the washed blue sky hovers like a hand painted bowl." Clearly, this guy took some creative writing seminars in college.

Meandering dirt paths connect five rock formations and a cliff dwelling. The puzzles are indigenous to the Anasazi world; success hinges on your keen observation of nature and its sounds. I recommend you press Control + J (or ⌘ + J in Macintosh version) and read the new pages in the professor's journal. The writing is compelling, and the professor is nice enough to include a rough map of the area.

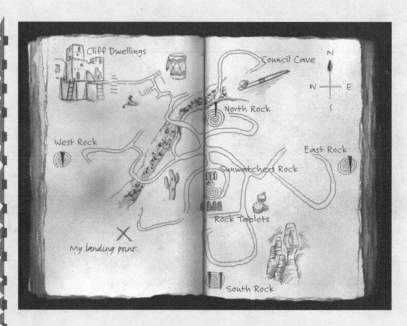

FIGURE 4-1. JOURNAL MAP

Arrival: Chasm Crossing

You jump through the time gate onto a scenic overlook. A crow rises from a tree stump and flies off down to the desert canyon below.

FIGURE 4-2. AS THE CROW FLIES. HERE'S WHERE YOU ARRIVE FOR YOUR ANASAZI ADVENTURE.

▲ Turn right to face the rock wall.

▲ Move forward four times to the log.

▲ Take the log. Why? Because it's there.

▲ Return to the dead stump and turn left down the path.

▲ Move forward five times (not six!) to the chasm.

You can't place the log in the chasm close-up. I tried this for a couple of weeks before I realized I had to back up a step first.

**FIGURE 4-3.
A LOG TOO FAR.**
GRAB THIS LOG AND
THROW IT ACROSS
THE CHASM.

▲ Drag the log and release it over the chasm to place it.

▲ Move forward across the chasm.

▲ Continue forward five moves to the path fork, then turn left to face the cliff dwelling.

FIGURE 4-4. CROSSROADS. ALL THE PATHS ORIGINATE HERE, LEADING OUT TO ROCK FORMATIONS, CAVERNS, AND CLIFF DWELLINGS.

▲ Move forward once.

▲ Turn left and take two steps forward to where another path branches to the right.

▲ Turn right and follow the path under the stone bridge.

▲ As you move under the bridge, that pesky Guardian might make an appearance and say something like, "You, like the other, will not escape your doom." Is that right? Tell me about it, static boy.

▲ Continue forward into the cavern.

FIGURE 4-5. RIVERBED TRAIL. TAKE THIS PATH UNDER THE STONE BRIDGE TO REACH COUNCIL CAVE.

Council Cave: Peace Pipe/Paw Print Puzzle

▲ Move through the outer room of the cavern.

▲ In the inner room, step up to the snake painting on the wall.

▲ For the quick solution to this puzzle, jump ahead to Figure 4-7. To understand the puzzle logic, read on.

▲ Turn left to face the circle painting.

Note that the circle has eight sections, each containing a different animal paw print. Note also the arrows in the circle's center pointing in the four compass directions. Each paw print corresponds to a compass direction. (See Figure 4-6.)

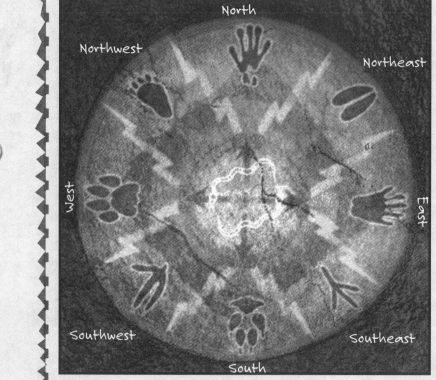

FIGURE 4-6. PAW COMPASS

▲ Turn right to face the snake painting again.

Circles run the length of the snake's body, and the same eight animal prints from the circle painting are located under the snake. Moving from circle to circle along the snake, notice that you're moving in the eight compass directions. Aha! The snake is a kind of map, and the paw compass is the map's legend.

Now look at the first circle, the one closest to the snake's head. To move to that circle from the snake's head, which compass direction must you move? The answer, of course, is to take a nap. Or you could say northeast. Either way, you're in good shape. Now check the circle painting again. Which paw glyph corresponds to the direction northeast? Yes, it's the deer hoofprint:

Now turn back to the snake painting.

▲ Click on the deer hoofprint (third from left) under the snake painting.

See how the deer hoofprint appears in the first circle? Starting at the head, you must fill the circles with the correct paws. The correct paw print for each circle will correspond to the direction you traveled from the previous circle. Here's the correct sequence:

FIGURE 4-7. GIVING PAWS. CLICK ON THE PAW PRINTS UNDER THE SNAKE IN THE ORDER THEY APPEAR IN THE SNAKE'S CIRCLES HERE, STARTING AT THE HEAD AND MOVING TOWARD THE TAIL.

▲ When you fill in the circles from head to tail correctly, the snake's tail rattles.

▲ Turn right and approach the smoking peace pipe.

▲ Click on the pipe to trigger an appearance by the spirit of an Anasazi shaman.

▲ When the shaman finishes telling each creation myth, click again. He tells five stories.

FIGURE 4-8. SHAMAN'S MESSAGE. HE WANTS TO TELL YOU ABOUT THE HISTORY OF CREATION, THE RISE OF CIVILIZATION, AND THE MYSTERIOUS DISAPPEARANCE OF HIS PEOPLE. KEEP CLICKING ON THE ROCK. HE TELLS FIVE STORIES.

These are the Anasazi shaman's five messages:

(Chants.) Greetings, children of the earth. I am the storyteller of my people, and I shall tell you of the history of creation. Before the physical manifestation of the world, there existed only the eternal Void. Then the Great Mystery, who is the source of all, breathed life into Grandfather Sun and Grandmother Moon. When this was done, Great Mystery rolled substance into a ball to form the earth. And the Earth Mother became home to countless forms of life.

Each living thing inherited its beauty, wisdom, love, equality, and wholeness, and understood its role in Great Mystery's divine plan. Yet the human tribe strayed from the righteous path, and three times the world was destroyed that evil might be purged. Only the people with good in their hearts reached this fourth world, and these began a great migration. So did our people come to these Canyon Lands, and here our culture flourished in harmony with Mother Earth.

As spring is the season of the rebirth, so came a time when the people were renewed. Great Mystery sent benefactors from a distant place, to join our council fire in the Canyon Lands. They offered to plant the Seed of Enrichment within our shaman, that it would come to fruit within the crop of his children. His descendants grew to possess great wisdom, as our benefactors had promised.

We built towering cities within the cliffs between the salt seas. Our artisans fashioned jewelry inlaid with the Blue Stone. Their works of fired clay were adorned with the rich colors of Mother Earth. Our irrigated mesas brimmed with squash and maize. And with the magic of the great gift, our wisdom grew and our spirits soared. So have the seeds of our benefactors enriched and renewed our people.

Our people made wise use of the gift. Our benefactors looked down, and were pleased with our people. So did they offer us a new world, there to live long lives of peace and plenty. Fearless did our people enter into the house of light. Their bodies had no weight, but floated as an eagle feather in the wind. They passed through Time, and came to land surrounded by a warm blue sea. From that land, they journeyed to the home of our benefactors. Thus did the people vanish from this land, and only their echoes remain in the desert canyons.

▲ Exit the caverns.

▲ Follow the path back under the stone bridge. Continue until you reach the intersection, then turn left on the main path.

▲ Move forward twice and turn right.

▲ Move forward once and turn left.

▲ Ascend the path up to Sunwatcher's Rock. (If you get lost, refer to the map in Figure 4-1.)

Sunwatcher's Rock: Sun Dagger Puzzle

A man-made rock formation hunkers at the top of the path. If you've read the professor's journal, you know this is an Anasazi solar calendar. In front, a lever juts from a rock podium. Pulling the lever activates a hidden mechanism that shifts rock slabs in the formation. The lever can be set in five positions.

▲ Pull the lever from setting to setting.

▲ After each setting, go forward two steps to look at the sun spiral etched in the rock wall. Note how the beam of light falling on the etching—the "sun dagger"—changes with each setting.

FIGURE 4-9. SUNWATCHER'S ROCK. YANK THAT LEVER AROUND AND WATCH THE ROCK SLABS SHIFT. THEN STEP FORWARD AND CHECK OUT THE SUN SPIRAL.

Straight up is the lever's neutral setting—no sun dagger shines on the sun spiral. The other four lever settings activate four puzzle mechanisms in the Anasazi world. Where are these puzzle mechanisms? Hey, what do you think this is, a cheat book? Don't worry, you'll get your answers. But let's discover the puzzles one at a time, following a natural, organic path, in the deepest sense of the Anasazi way. Chant with me now: Ahe, ahe, ahe, ooooh. OK, I'm getting carried away.

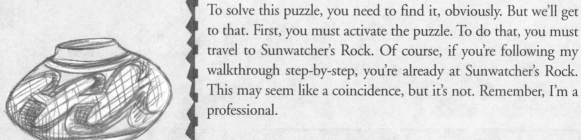

West Rock: Handprint Puzzle

To solve this puzzle, you need to find it, obviously. But we'll get to that. First, you must activate the puzzle. To do that, you must travel to Sunwatcher's Rock. Of course, if you're following my walkthrough step-by-step, you're already at Sunwatcher's Rock. This may seem like a coincidence, but it's not. Remember, I'm a professional.

▲ Go to Sunwatcher's Rock.

▲ Pull the lever all the way to the left. (See Figure 4-10.)

FIGURE 4-10. TO ACTIVATE WEST ROCK PUZZLE: MOVE THE LEVER AT SUNWATCHER'S ROCK ALL THE WAY LEFT TO DIRECT THE "SUN DAGGER" OVER THE SPIRAL SUN GLYPH AS SHOWN HERE.

Now let's go find the West Rock. Refer to the map in Figure 4-1 or follow the directions below:

▲ From Sunwatcher's Rock, go back down the path to the intersection (nine moves) and turn right to face the cliff dwelling.

▲ Take one step forward and turn left.

▲ Follow the path over the stone bridge until you can't go forward anymore. (You should see the other stone bridge up ahead.)

▲ Turn left and take two steps to the rock wall.

If you turn left here, you see another spiral sun etched on a rock. Note the sun dagger. If you weren't cheating with my book, this would be your clue to recreate this "West Rock" etching back at Sunwatcher's Rock with the lever mechanism. Ha! Don't you pity the poor fools trying to figure out this stuff on their own?

FIGURE 4-11. WEST ROCK CLUE. THIS SUN SPIRAL WITH ITS SUN DAGGER TIPS YOU OFF TO THE PROPER SETTING BACK AT SUNWATCHER'S ROCK.

▲ Turn right at the rock wall and go forward to the small cave.

▲ Enter the cave.

▲ Inside, take two steps forward and turn right. Heed the voice that speaks: "There is value in the shadows."

▲ Find and take the flashlight.

FIGURE 4-12. SHAKY LIGHT SOURCE. THIS THING IS HANDY, BUT NOT TOO RELIABLE. CHECK THE PROFESSOR'S JOURNAL FOR TIPS ON USING IT.

▲ Step back, turn left, and step forward to the dark alcove in the wall.

▲ Turn left again to face a second dark alcove.

This next part is kind of fun. Remember what the professor said about his flashlight in the journal? He wrote: "I had to shake the thing to get any light at all. The batteries must be corroded."

▲ Grab the flashlight—that is, click and hold on it—then drag it over the dark alcove.

▲ Still holding down the mouse button, jiggle the mouse forward and back to "shake" the flashlight. Keep the flashlight over the dark alcove!

After a few jiggles, the flashlight flickers on and off several times. Look quickly at the carved glyphs the light reveals. Or not. It doesn't matter, really, because I include screen shots of the carvings for you here.

FIGURE 4-13. OUT OF THE SHADOWS, LEFT SIDE. YOUR BALKY FLASHLIGHT EVENTUALLY REVEALS THIS SET OF CAVE GLYPHS IN THE LEFT ALCOVE. THE ORDER FROM LEFT TO RIGHT IS IMPORTANT.

▲ Turn to face the shadowy alcove on the right.

▲ Grab the flashlight and move it over the alcove.

▲ As before, shake the flashlight until it flickers on.

▲ Shine the light on the four petroglyphs carved in the wall.

FIGURE 4-14. OUT OF THE SHADOWS, RIGHT SIDE. AND
HERE ARE THE GLYPHS FROM THE RIGHT ALCOVE.

▲ Exit the cave.

▲ Go forward past the sun dagger etching as far as you can.

▲ Turn left and approach the hand painting on the wall.

▲ Click on glyphs following the sequence you found in the cave. Here's how:

1. First, click on the glyphs in the left-to-right sequence shown in Figure 4-13.

2. Second, click on the glyphs in the left-to-right sequence shown in Figure 4-14.

▲ Watch a coyote shadow appear and howl. After it disappears, turn left.

▲ Click on the small sun spiral: It's an entry button.

FIGURE 4-15. WORTH A HOWL. HERE'S THE FINISHED HANDPRINT PUZZLE, COMPLETE WITH COYOTE SHADOW. NOW TURN LEFT AND PUSH THE ENTRY BUTTON.

- ▲ Turn right to see the now-open secret chamber.

- ▲ Enter the secret chamber: It's a spectacular, gigantic geode with crystalline walls.

- ▲ Inside the chamber, step forward, then turn right.

- ▲ Watch the large Sun Glyph rise from the water. Note your surroundings carefully, including that dripping sound. This information will be important later.

FIGURE 4-16. SUN GLYPH. QUITE A SIGHT TO SEE. BUT YOU'D BETTER LISTEN, TOO.

East Rock: Squirrel and Acorn Puzzle

- ▲ Go back to Sunwatcher's Rock.

- ▲ Move the lever to the second position from the left. (See Figure 4-17.)

Tip
Aside from the obvious Sun Glyph, note two other important clues from the West Rock area—the coyote (your "spirit guide"), and the sound of dripping water coming from the secret chamber.

FIGURE 4-17. TO ACTIVATE EAST ROCK PUZZLE: MOVE THE
LEVER AT SUNWATCHER'S ROCK TO THE SECOND POSITION
FROM THE LEFT. THIS DIRECTS THE SUN DAGGER OVER THE
SUN SPIRAL GLYPH AS SHOWN HERE.

Now let's seek out East Rock. Refer to the map in Figure 4-1
or follow the directions below:

▲ From Sunwatcher's Rock, go back down the path to the
   intersection (nine moves) and turn right to face the cliff
   dwelling.

▲ Take one step forward and turn right.

▲ Follow the path to the end. You should face an acorn-
   embossed rock wall.

▲ Turn left and take the stick.

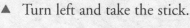

FIGURE 4-18. SPEAK SOFTLY, AND ... YOU NEVER KNOW
WHEN YOU'LL NEED A GOOD STICK.

▲ Turn again to face the path.

▲ Move forward three times and turn left. You should see a
path leading up a rocky hillside.

▲ Climb the rocky path. And speaking of Rocky: When you
see the squirrel, follow it.

FIGURE 4-19. WHAT
A NUTTY SQUIRREL!
THAT LITTLE GUY IS
YOUR SPIRIT GUIDE.
FOLLOW HIM TO
THE TREE AND
ROCK. HE WANTS TO
SHOW YOU WHERE
HE HIDES HIS FOOD.

On the way up, note that you pass another sun spiral, this one with the East Rock sun dagger on it. You also see a hive full of busy, buzzing bees. Don't touch it!

FIGURE 4-20. EVERY
MOVE YOU MAKE.
GET IT? STING? NEVER
MIND. JUST DON'T
TOUCH THAT HIVE OR
YOU'LL GET A FACEFUL
OF MAD BEE. USE THE
STICK INSTEAD.

▲ Continue up the path to the dead tree. The squirrel picks up an acorn, jumps from the tree, and drops the acorn in a crack in the rock.

▲ Step forward to the rock to see a close-up of the acorn in the crack.

Uh-oh. That acorn's wedged in there tight. Now what? You could try to dig it out with the stick, but it'll just rattle around. You need some sort of adhesive substance. Is there anything sticky nearby?

FIGURE 4-21. NUTS! IT'S STUCK. WHAT YOU NEED IS A STICKY STICK.

▲ Go back down the hill to the beehive.

▲ Poke the beehive with the stick. A bit of honey drips out.

▲ Jab the tip of the stick into the honey. Some honey stays on the tip of the stick.

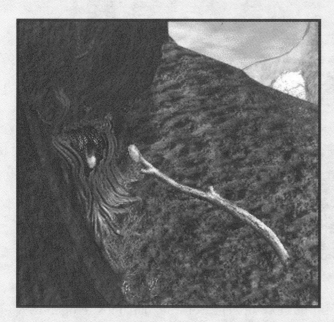

FIGURE 4-22. LOOK, HONEY! NOW THINGS WILL STICK
TO THIS STICK.

▲ Go back up the hill to the acorn.

▲ Use the stick to pull out the acorn. The stick disappears,
  and the acorn replaces it in your inventory.

▲ Go back down the hill to the acorn-embossed rock wall.

▲ Place the squirrel's acorn on the wall's embossed acorn.

▲ Enter the secret chamber.

▲ Step forward to the baskets to get a close-up of a matchbox.

FIGURE 4-23. GOT A MATCH? YES, AS A MATTER OF FACT.

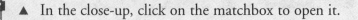

▲ In the close-up, click on the matchbox to open it.

▲ Click on the matchbox again to get a match. The match moves to the corner of the screen.

▲ Take two steps back and turn right to face the fire pit.

▲ Click and hold on the match.

▲ Drag the match over the stone with the cutout figure. This lights the match. (Don't release the mouse button after lighting the match, or the match will drop. Then you'll have to get a new match and try again.)

▲ Hold the lit match over the wood in the fire pit.

▲ After the wood catches fire, turn left twice to see the Standing Person Glyph projected onto the far wall. Cool!

▲ Listen to the crackling fire too.

FIGURE 4-24. ANCIENT FLICK. LIGHT THE WOOD IN THE FIRE
PIT TO PROJECT THE GLYPH ONTO THE FAR WALL.

See the pattern yet? Rock formations lie in four directions, each marked by its own sun spiral glyph. To activate each location, you must set the sun dagger mechanism at Sunwatcher's Rock to match the location's sun spiral. At each location, you solve a puzzle, meet a spirit guide (an animal), open a secret chamber, find a big glyph, and hear a unique sound.

North Rock: Feather Headdress Puzzle

▲ Go back to Sunwatcher's Rock.

▲ Move the lever to the second position from the right. (See Figure 4-25.)

Tip
Aside from the obvious Standing Person Glyph, note two other important clues from the East Rock area—the squirrel (your spirit guide), and the sound of the crackling fire in the secret chamber.

FIGURE 4-25. TO ACTIVATE NORTH ROCK PUZZLE: MOVE THE LEVER AT SUNWATCHER'S ROCK TO THE SECOND POSITION FROM THE RIGHT. THIS DIRECTS THE SUN DAGGER OVER THE SUN SPIRAL, AS SHOWN HERE.

And off we go to North Rock. Refer to the map in Figure 4-1 or follow these directions:

▲ From Sunwatcher's Rock, go back down the path to the intersection (nine moves) and turn right to face the cliff dwelling.

▲ Take three steps forward and grab the feather on the rock.

Did you hear the sound? That was a woodpecker—pecking wood, I assume. You just picked up a woodpecker feather. Admire it. Enjoy it. You're going to lose it in a second.

FIGURE 4-26. WOODPECKER FEATHER. HOW CAN YOU TELL?
LISTEN TO THE SOUND WHEN YOU PICK IT UP.

▲ Turn right and take a step forward. A crow (another spirit guide) caws at you and flies up the path.

▲ Take another step forward and note the sun spiral. (Don't worry about the scorpion.)

▲ Turn around to look back down the path.

▲ See that light-colored feather at the far right? Take it.

Did you hear the owl? This is an owl feather. Notice that it replaced your woodpecker feather. Apparently, you are so weakened by excitement that you can carry only one feather at a time. Or maybe these are magic feathers, and so they're really heavy. I'm not sure. I didn't have the guts to ask the game designers at GTE Entertainment about this feather business. Actually, the answer is that you can only carry one item at a time in inventory (with the exception of the Gene Pod).

▲ Take two steps forward and turn right. Hey, there's the woodpecker feather, right back in its original place.

▲ Take the woodpecker feather again. The owl feather returns to its original place.

Of course, this little exchange was totally unnecessary. I wanted to make an educational point. It's also therapeutic to waste time on occasion. I'm just helping you become a better person.

▲ Turn right and go to the end of the path. You should see a bunch of birds frolicking on a rock up ahead.

▲ Turn left and go forward to the empty headdress-shaped stone.

This headdress is clearly in need of feathers. You have one—a woodpecker feather. But in which slot should you place it?

▲ Back up and turn to the bird etchings on the wall.

▲ Note the order from left to right—turkey, owl, crow, quail, woodpecker.

Tip
You can store up to three feathers in front of the headdress stone. Of course, you won't need to if you're following this walkthrough.

FIGURE 4-27. BIRDS OF A FEATHER, PART 1. NOTE THE ORDER OF THE BIRDS FROM LEFT TO RIGHT—TURKEY, OWL, CROW, QUAIL, WOODPECKER. MIGHT THAT MATCH THE FEATHER ORDER ON THE HEADDRESS STONE?

- ▲ Approach the headdress stone.

- ▲ Place the woodpecker feather in its slot according to the wall etching—farthest right.

- ▲ Back away from the headdress stone and turn around.

- ▲ Go forward four times and get the crow feather.

- ▲ Bring the crow feather to the headdress stone and put it in the center slot.

- ▲ Turn around, go forward four times, and turn right.

- ▲ Take one step forward and get the turkey feather.

- ▲ Bring the turkey feather to the headdress stone, and place it in the left-most slot.

- ▲ Retrieve the owl feather from the bottom of the path and bring it back.

- ▲ Put the owl feather in its place—second from the left.

- ▲ Return to the bottom of the path (to the rock where you found the woodpecker feather) and turn left.

- ▲ Take two steps forward and turn left.

- ▲ Take two more steps forward. This is the path to the South Rock area. A voice says, "I know what you seek." (Translation: You're getting warmer, man.)

- ▲ After you hear the voice, take two more steps forward and turn left. There it is!

Note

You need five feathers, but seven lay in various locations. Two are red herrings—the blue jay feather under the stone bridge, and the mourning dove feather near the log over the chasm.

FIGURE 4-28. QUAIL FEATHER. YOU HAD TO DO SOME
SEARCHING, BUT HERE'S THAT DARN QUAIL FEATHER.

▲ Take the quail feather back to the headdress stone and put
it in the remaining slot (second from right).

▲ Click on the feather button above the headdress stone.
Watch the stone transform into a gorgeous, real feathered
headdress.

FIGURE 4-29. BIRDS OF A FEATHER, PART 2. HERE'S THE
CORRECT PLACEMENT ORDER FOR THE BIRD FEATHERS.

▲ Back up and turn left to see the now-open secret chamber.

▲ Enter the chamber.

▲ Approach the bird statue. Note it well, and listen well.

Tip
Aside from the obvious
Bird Glyph, note two other
important clues from the
North Rock area—the
crow (your spirit guide
here), and the sound of
the rustling leaves in the
secret chamber.

FIGURE 4-30. BIRD GLYPH. NICE BEAK. WONDER HOW ALL
THOSE LEAVES GOT HERE? LISTEN TO THEM RUSTLE.

South Rock: Bow-and-Arrow Puzzle

▲ Go back to Sunwatcher's Rock.

▲ Move the lever all the way to the right. (See Figure 4-31.)

FIGURE 4-31. TO ACTIVATE SOUTH ROCK PUZZLE: MOVE THE LEVER AT SUNWATCHER'S ROCK ALL THE WAY TO THE RIGHT. THIS DIRECTS THE SUN DAGGER OVER THE SUN SPIRAL AS SHOWN HERE.

Now let's check out the South Rock puzzle. Refer to the map in Figure 4-1 or follow these directions:

▲ From Sunwatcher's Rock, go back down the path to the intersection (nine moves) and turn right to face the cliff dwelling.

▲ Take one step forward and turn right.

▲ Move forward four times and turn right to face down a path. Note the needle spire in the distance.

▲ Move ahead five times and pick up the arrowhead on the right side of the path. The arrowhead moves to the corner of the screen.

▲ Continue forward to the end of the path and turn left.

Whoa! Did you see that hawk? Another spirit guide. Watch where it flies—right through the needle-like opening at the top of that distant tower. What's the message here? He certainly doesn't expect us to load that bow with an arrow, add an arrowhead, and shoot the darn thing through the opening, does he?

FIGURE 4-32. HAWK AND BOW. BOY, THAT'S A BIG BIRD. WATCH WHERE IT FLIES TO DISCOVER YOUR TARGET.

To shoot arrows with the bow:

▲ Step forward to the bow.

▲ Click on the bow to load an arrow.

▲ Click on the arrowhead to put it on the arrow's tip.

▲ Click and hold on the bowstring, then pull it back.

▲ Release the mouse button to shoot the arrow.

FIGURE 4-33. AIM AND LISTEN. AIM FOR THAT HOLE AT THE TOP OF THE TOWER—AND DON'T SHOOT TILL THE WIND KICKS UP.

You get three shots per arrowhead. Chances are you won't put it through on the first round of three, so you'll have to search for more arrowheads.

If you need more arrowheads:

▲ Back away from the bow and turn left.

▲ Move forward four times down the path to the rock with the painting of the hunter shooting a deer. We'll call this the "hunting rock."

▲ Pick up the arrowhead and return to the bow.

FIGURE 4-34. HUNTING ROCK. UNDER THIS ROCK YOU'LL FIND AN ENDLESS SUPPLY OF ARROWHEADS. REMEMBER, EACH ARROWHEAD YOU PICK UP IS ACTUALLY THREE ARROWHEADS.

If you just fire away at the target, you'll notice that most of your shots fall short. At some point you'll hear the shaman's voice: "Shoot straight as the wind blows." This is critical advice. Hear the wind blowing? It gusts loudly for a second or two, grows quiet for 15 or 20 seconds, gains power again for a moment, and so on. Wait until the wind is blowing the weakest. Select the first arrowhead (of the three available) and line up your shot slightly to the left of the hole you're shooting for. Pull the bow back as far as it will go and release the arrow. (Note, I am assuming you are running in 640 by 480 resolution.)

Listen carefully to the wind. When it gusts loudest, shoot an arrow straight for the target.

- ▲ Shoot arrows at the target and, if necessary, return to the "hunting rock" for more arrowheads until you finally zing one through the tower opening.

- ▲ After your successful shot, back away from the bow and turn around. You should see the hawk fly into the now-open secret chamber up ahead.

- ▲ Go to the secret chamber and enter.

- ▲ Approach the Buffalo Glyph on the wall and watch it transform into a thundering herd.

Tip
Aside from the obvious Buffalo Glyph, note two other important clues from the South Rock area—the hawk (your spirit guide), and the sound of the thundering herd in the secret chamber.

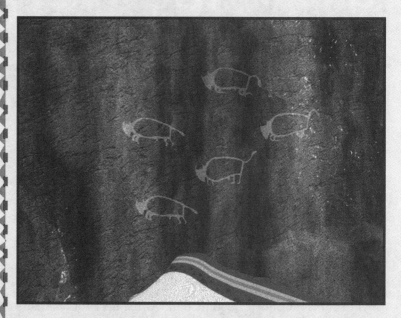

FIGURE 4-35. BUFFALO GLYPH. INTERESTING TRANSFORMA-
TION. AS ALWAYS, LOOK AND LISTEN.

Behind Sunwatcher's Rock: Stone Tablets Puzzle

- ▲ Go back to Sunwatcher's Rock.

- ▲ Move the lever straight up. (See Figure 4-36.)

FIGURE 4-36. TO ACTIVATE THE STONE TABLETS PUZZLE:
MOVE THE LEVER AT SUNWATCHER'S ROCK STRAIGHT UP SO
NO SUN DAGGERS SHINE ON THE SUN SPIRAL.

Now refer to the map in Figure 4-1 or follow these directions:

▲ From Sunwatcher's Rock, go back down the path to the intersection (nine moves) and turn right to face the cliff dwelling.

▲ Take one step forward and turn right.

▲ Move forward four times and turn right. You should face down a path and see the needle spire in the distance.

▲ Go forward four times, then take the path that branches off to the right.

▲ Follow the path to the end.

▲ Turn right to face the stone tablets.

You'll find these tablets just behind Sunwatcher's Rock. First, note the sun-spiral glyph at the top of each tablet. It designates one of the four rock formations—North, South, East, West (going left to right)—where you just solved puzzles. Now look at the other glyphs.

▲ Click on various glyphs and listen to the sounds.

Many of these sounds should be familiar. Some are animals. Remember your spirit guides? There was one for each puzzle, wasn't there? Other sounds should be familiar, too—water dripping, fire crackling, and so on. In each of the four secret chambers, you heard a distinctive sound. OK, enough coy hints.

To solve the stone tablets puzzle: Each tablet represents one of the four rock formations. The sun dagger(s) on each tablet's sun spiral indicates which rock formation it represents. On each tablet, you must click on two glyphs—one that represents that location's spirit guide, and one that represents that location's secret-chamber sound. (Figure 4-37 shows the completed puzzle.)

▲ On the North Rock tablet (farthest left), click on the crow and the leaf.

▲ On the South Rock tablet (second from left), click on the hawk and the thunderstorm.

▲ On the East Rock tablet (second from right), click on the squirrel and the fire.

▲ On the West Rock tablet (farthest right), click on the coyote and the water droplets.

FIGURE 4-37. STONE TABLETS SOLUTION

▲ Once you've highlighted all the correct glyphs, click on the sun-spiral button above the stone tablets to open the secret chamber.

▲ Enter the secret chamber.

Gene Pod Chamber

▲ Approach the podium to get a close-up of the Anasazi Gene Pod.

▲ Click on the Gene Pod to see the message. When the message ends, the Gene Pod automatically appears in your inventory.

FIGURE 4-38. ANASAZI GENE POD. ONCE YOU OPEN THE FINAL CHAMBER, ENTER AND SNAG THE GENE POD.

▲ Exit the chamber.

▲ Retrace your steps to the crossroads in front of the cave dwelling.

▲ Turn toward the cave dwelling.

▲ Follow the winding path up to cactus garden at the cliff dwelling's base.

Base of Cliff Dwelling: Corn/Cacti Puzzle

▲ Go to the far end of the cactus garden and pick up the broken arrow.

▲ Turn to the ear of corn stuck in the ground.

FIGURE 4-39. BATES SPECIAL. ARE YOU FEELING PSYCHO? GRAB THIS BROKEN ARROW AND START STABBING STUFF.

▲ Click once on the arrow in your inventory slot. The arrow becomes your cursor.

▲ Move the arrow over any of the cacti and then click to stab holes. All of the water can be found at the base of each cacti. Water trickles from cactus holes and the ear of corn grows.

▲ Keep poking holes in the cacti until the cornstalk grows past the top of the wall. (The ear needs five drinks of water.)

▲ Go forward to climb the cornstalk.

FIGURE 4-40. JACK AND THE CORNSTALK. HACK AWAY AT THE CACTI TO WATER THE EAR OF CORN. SOON YOU HAVE A CORNSTALK LADDER.

Cliff Dwelling Entrance: Rattlesnake Puzzle

▲ From the top of the cornstalk, take two steps forward.

▲ Turn right and take the rattle from the basket.

▲ Turn around to face the rattlesnake.

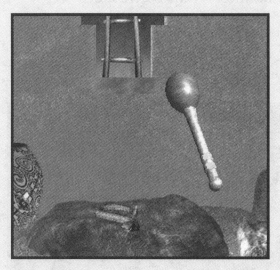

FIGURE 4-41.
RATTLE AND
RATTLESNAKE.
THE SNAKE
RATTLES A
GREETING. CAN
YOU RESPOND IN
KIND? GRAB THE
RATTLE AND
GIVE IT A SHAKE.

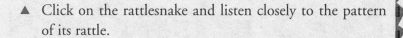

▲ Click on the rattlesnake and listen closely to the pattern of its rattle.

▲ Click on the rattle and shake it in the same pattern.

This may be a little tricky. I managed to match the snake's rattle on my first try, but I had to really jerk the mouse to get the rattle going.

▲ Once you correctly repeat the pattern of the rattlesnake's rattle, the snake turns into a ladder. Climb it.

▲ Climb the next ladder as well.

▲ Turn right to face the loom.

Loom Room: Blanket-Weave Puzzle

Here's an original (and perhaps perplexing) puzzle. The object here is to weave an Anasazi blanket. In the following steps, refer to Figure 4-42:

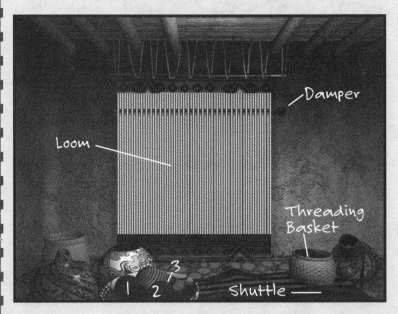

FIGURE 4-42. ANASAZI LOOM

1. Drag the shuttle stick over the threading basket and release. The shuttle drops into the basket.

2. Drag yarn ball number 1 to the threading basket and release.

3. Click on yarn ball number 1 to pull out the end of the yarn.

4. Click on the shuttle to thread the yarn through it.

5. Click on the loom to string the yarn.

6. Click on the damper to weave the bottom third of the blanket.

7. Repeat steps 2 through 6 using yarn ball number 2.

8. Repeat steps 2 through 6 using yarn ball number 3.

9. When you've completed the blanket, note the glowing Cornstalk Glyph.

FIGURE 4-43. CORNSTALK GLYPH. WEAVE A BLANKET, GET A GLYPH. NOT A BAD DEAL.

▲ After you complete the loom puzzle, turn left to face the wall.

▲ Move backwards to climb down both ladders.

▲ On the ground floor (at the bottom of the snake ladder), turn left.

▲ Go forward through the window and turn right.

▲ Climb the ladder.

▲ Enter the Drum Room.

Drum Room: Drum & Chimes Puzzle

▲ Find and take the drumstick.

▲ Turn to the chimes.

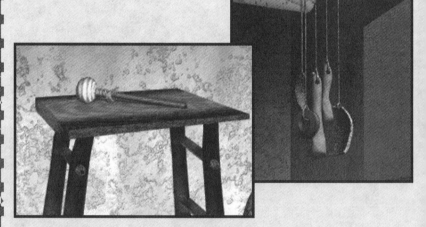

FIGURE 4-44. LET'S MAKE MUSIC. YOU NEED A GOOD EAR TO SOLVE THIS PUZZLE. CLICK ON THE CHIMES, LISTEN TO THE SONG, GRAB THE DRUMSTICK, AND REPEAT THE SONG ON THE DRUMS. GOOD LUCK.

▲ Click on the chimes and listen carefully to its five-note "song." (Repeat as many times as necessary.)

▲ Use the drumstick to repeat the five-note chime song on the drums. (Figure 4-45 shows the order.)

FIGURE 4-45. DRUM SOLUTION. USE THE DRUMSTICK TO BEAT ONCE ON EACH DRUM IN THE ORDER SHOWN HERE.

▲ Turn right to see the now-open secret passage.

▲ Enter the Shaman Room.

Shaman Room: Niche & Rag Puzzle

▲ Go forward to the fire pit.

▲ Take the stick.

▲ Turn to the five niches in the wall. Don't touch them!

If you try to explore any of the five niches with your hand cursor, fanged creatures attack and blind you temporarily. Until you cast some light on the niches, all five contain only venomous creatures.

FIGURE 4-46. ANCIENT RAG. DON'T STICK YOUR HAND IN DARK PLACES. INSTEAD, USE THE GLOWING STICK TO LIGHT THE WAY. THEN GRAB THAT RAG.

▲ Move the glowing stick over each niche.

▲ When you find the rag, release the stick and take the rag. The rag replaces the stick in your inventory.

▲ Turn around to face the opposite wall.

▲ Dip the rag in the stone bucket of water.

▲ Use the wet rag on the wall to wipe away dirt and reveal the Shaman Glyph.

FIGURE 4-47. SHAMAN GLYPH. WIPE THE WALL WITH A WET
RAG TO SEE THIS IMPORTANT PIECE OF INFORMATION.

▲ Return to the drum room and face the ladder. See that leaf
imprint on the right side of the doorway? Remember it.

▲ Face the drums and back away from them to descend the
ladder.

▲ At the bottom of the ladder, turn right and exit through
the window.

▲ Take two more steps forward and turn right.

▲ Step forward and turn right to the sand-spiral pattern.

Kiva Entry: Sand-Spiral Puzzle

Approach the sand and watch the leaves and pine cones blow onto the spiral pattern. Extra items land in a pile left of the pattern. Three empty spots appear at the end of the spiral. You must choose items from the pile and place them in the empty spots to complete the sequence.

Note the sequence of items lining the spiral, starting at its center—green leaf, red leaf, red-tipped white leaf, yellow maple leaf, green leaf, pine cone, orange leaf. The next item, a green maple leaf, marks a central position, because after it, the previous sequence reverses—orange leaf, pine cone, green leaf, yellow maple. Thus, the three empty spaces should be filled in the reverse order of the first (innermost) three items in the spiral pattern.

▲ Starting with the empty slot next to the yellow maple leaf, place these three items in order—red-tipped white leaf, red leaf, green leaf.

▲ Step back and take the yellow maple leaf from the stone basin above the sand puzzle.

Note
This puzzle will not activate unless you have the Anasazi Gene Pod.

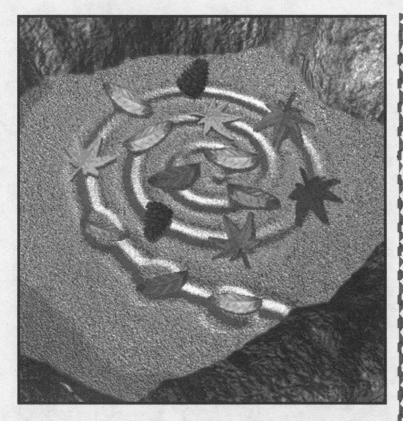

FIGURE 4-48. COLORLESS SOLUTION. THEY SAY A PICTURE IS WORTH A THOUSAND WORDS. BUT THIS ONE'S NOT IN COLOR, SO A FEW WORDS ARE NECESSARY. TO FILL THE EMPTY PUZZLE SLOTS (LEFT TO RIGHT), CHOOSE THE RED-TIPPED WHITE LEAF, THE RED LEAF, AND THE GREEN LEAF.

▲ Return to the Drum Room.

▲ Turn around to face the door.

▲ Put the yellow leaf onto the leaf imprint on the right side of the Drum Room door. Across the rooftop, a secret door opens to the kiva.

▲ Enter the kiva.

Kiva: Final Puzzle

After you enter the kiva, look around the room. Lot of glyphs, eh? But all your earlier exploration and puzzle-solving pays off here.

Remember that the reward for solving most of the earlier puzzles was access to a symbol of some sort, usually a glyph—sun, buffalo, cornstalk, etc. Including the Bee Glyph on the Gene Pod, you found seven large symbols. You must activate all seven of those special glyphs (and only those seven) on the three walls of this kiva.

Turn to the left wall and click on the Bird Glyph (from North Rock) and the Cornstalk Glyph (from the Loom Room).

FIGURE 4-49. KIVA LEFT WALL

FIGURE 4-50. KIVA BACK WALL

Turn left again and click on the Standing Person Glyph (from East Rock), the Sun Glyph (from West Rock), and the Shaman Glyph (from the Shaman Room).

FIGURE 4-51. KIVA RIGHT WALL

Turn left again and click on the Buffalo Glyph (from South Rock) and the Bee Glyph (from the Gene Pod).

Turn left one more time and click on the center of the ceremonial circle. After the secret entrance opens, move forward to get on the ladder, then move backward to climb down the ladder.

FIGURE 4-52.
KIVA FRONT
WALL

Time Gate: Transportal Room

At the bottom of the ladder, turn around and proceed down the passage to the transportal device. Do you suppose the professor has anything more to say? Approach the orb and find out. Then it's off to the next adventure:

▲ Click on the middle button. You'll see a spinning animation of a shimmering underwater city in the orb.

▲ Click on the orb to travel to Atlantis.

FIGURE 4-53. ATLANTIS FLYBY. NEXT STOP,
THE LAND DOWN UNDER.

Atlantis overvie[w]

I was not s[u...]
Enlightenme[nt...]
to other cult[ure...]

Building Three
Building Four
Central Building
Building Two
Building One

CHAPTER 5
Atlantis

TIMELAPSE'S FABULOUS ATLANTEAN WORLD is an under-sea complex encased in a protective dome, the surviving core of a once-glorious island continent. Video holograms throughout the complex provide information about the history and technology of Atlantis. You learn that the entire domed complex is actually an Atlantean outpost ship deployed long ago from a massive colonizing vessel. You also confront your shadowy tormentor, the Guardian. (No wonder he's so ticked off.)

Note
You can visit Atlantis only after you acquire Gene Pods from the Egypt, Anasazi, and Maya locations.

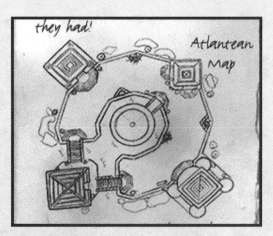

FIGURE 5-1. JOURNAL MAP. THE PROFESSOR KINDLY PROVIDES A SKETCHED MAP OF THE ATLANTEAN UNDERSEA COMPLEX IN HIS JOURNAL.

Arrival: Exploring the Outer Temples

You arrive on a walkway of liquid-black marble before a building that resembles a futuristic Egyptian pyramid. Overhead, a dome of raw particle energy holds back the ocean. Ambient light passing through this watery filter casts the city in an aqua glow. Again, the professor describes it best in his journal: "It's like waking up in the center of an emerald."

FIGURE 5-2. ATLANTIS ARRIVAL. YOU MATERIALIZE ON A
SIDEWALK ABOUT 20,000 LEAGUES UNDER THE SEA.

▲ Upon arrival, turn left and take two steps forward.

▲ Turn right and move forward through the doors of the
Egyptian-like pyramid.

Building One

Wow! These Atlanteans had great stuff. I mean, Americans have
good stuff, but not like this. Some of it's incomprehensible—you
click on things, they light up, then nothing happens—but that's
OK. It looks cool.

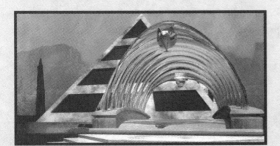

FIGURE 5-3.
BUILDING ONE

▲ Take a step into the room, turn right and approach the video kiosk.

▲ Touch the kiosk to trigger a video presentation.

This kiosk contains a pair of videos. The first video discusses the vessel's "surface escape modules." The host says you enable these escape pods at a main control panel. And where might that be?

 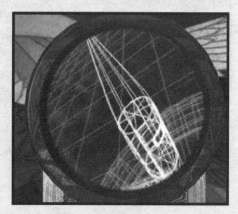

FIGURE 5-4. POD LADY. LISTEN TO WHAT SHE SAYS ABOUT ESCAPE PODS.

The second video discusses Atlantean time-gate technology. It warns that although these temporal gates are highly stable, they can collapse during transport of certain metals. Note the images displayed when the host speaks of transportal implosions—yes, the very Gene Pods you have in your possession. Big clue.

FIGURE 5-5. GATE CRASHER. HEED HER WARNING ABOUT "HOME WORLD" METALS (LIKE GENE POD CASINGS) THAT DESTROY TIME GATES. YOU WOULDN'T WANT THAT TO HAPPEN TO YOU.

▲ Turn around and go to the video kiosk on the opposite side of the room.

▲ Touch the kiosk to trigger a video presentation.

This second kiosk contains another pair of videos. The first one discusses the Atlantean "variable energy beam tool" responsible for the seemingly impossible engineering feats of the Mayan and Egyptian pyramids, the precision excavation for the Anasazi cliff dwellings, and the massive *Moai* stone heads on Easter Island. Note the reference to an access code and the minimum power setting.

FIGURE 5-6. ENERGY BEAM TOOL. GET ONE OF THESE FOR YOUR TOOL BELT. YOU'LL NEVER HAVE TO RENT A CRANE AGAIN.

The second video discusses the "star travel stasis pod." The host says that to initiate the stasis process, the code panel must be fully set, and the field generating base must sense the presence of an occupant. She also notes an interesting scenario: "Where environmental danger is imminent, the pod's code panel may be fully preset, leaving its system in a ready state."

FIGURE 5-7. STASIS PRIMER. WOULDN'T IT BE FUN TO PUSH A
GUY INTO A STASIS POD AND PUT HIM TO SLEEP FOR, LIKE,
A MILLION YEARS? IT'D HAVE TO BE SOMEBODY
UNPLEASANT, OF COURSE.

▲ Back away from the kiosk and turn left.

▲ Note carefully the glyph displayed on both sides of the
door.

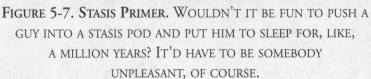

FIGURE 5-8. ATLANTEAN GRAFFITI. THAT GLYPH BY THE
DOOR MUST BE IMPORTANT, OR IT WOULDN'T BE
SO DARNED BIG.

▲ Exit Building One.

▲ Cross the far bridge and enter Building Two, the Mayan-
looking step pyramid.

Building Two

The first thing you see inside is a fountain topped with a stunning dolphin sculpture.

FIGURE 5-9.
BUILDING TWO

▲ Step to the middle of the room and turn right.

▲ Approach the video kiosk.

▲ Touch the kiosk to trigger the video.

This video discusses the assembly of the "basic synthetic servant" and its need for regular rejuicing at a beamed energy charging station. Do you think the Guardian has one of those in the complex?

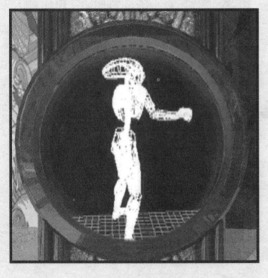

FIGURE 5-10.
THE GUARDIAN.
THERE HE IS.
EVEN IN
WIREFRAME, HE'S
ANNOYING.
WHERE'S HIS
CHARGING
STATION?

▲ Turn around and go to the video kiosk on the opposite side of the room.

▲ Touch the kiosk to trigger another video presentation.

This second kiosk speaks of the vast geothermal ocean of molten rock beneath the planet's surface, and how the Atlanteans have learned to harness this furnace of unimaginable power. They've also mastered solar, wind, and hydropower. They even know all the words to "Louie, Louie." And they want to pass this knowledge on to humans. Maybe they'll throw in milk and cookies, too. But we have to be very, very good. No fighting, no tantrums.

In any case, sounds like it might be good to get one of those laminate crystals.

FIGURE 5-11. KNOW-IT-ALLS. OK, OK, SO YOU KNOW EVERYTHING. BUT CAN YOU DO THE "MACARENA"?

▲ Back away from the kiosk and turn right to face the fountain.

▲ Carefully note the glyph on either side of the fountain.

FIGURE 5-12. FOUNTAIN OF KNOWLEDGE. YOU CAN LEARN A LOT BY STARING AT WATER. BUT IN THIS CASE, LET YOUR EYES WANDER TO THOSE GLYPHS.

▲ Exit Building Two.

▲ Take two steps forward.

▲ Turn left and approach Building Three, the one with the diamond-shaped tower on top.

▲ Enter Building Three.

Building Three

This structure is actually the communications center for the outpost ship. Inside, you find what looks like a big serving platter atop a two-legged podium. Believe it or not, this is actually a communications console.

FIGURE 5-13. BUILDING THREE

▲ Approach the communications console.

▲ Touch the center of the console screen to trigger a series of transmissions between the outpost crew (including the Guardian) and the Atlantean home world.

From these transmissions, you learn that this "Terran outpost" was trapped by surface storms, so the crew entered stasis chambers to wait for the atmosphere to clear. They programmed a synthetic servant—the Guardian—to oversee outpost operations and revive the crew when planetary conditions permitted a launch. But something went wrong. A massive electrical discharge damaged the A.I. (Artificial Intelligence) of the Guardian, who then refused to execute the full-scale self-destruct sequence ordered by the Atlantean home world.

FIGURE 5-14. PHONE HOME. VIEW THIS CHILLING SERIES OF
TRANSMISSIONS. LOOKS LIKE THE GUARDIAN HAS GONE NUTS.
AS IF YOU DIDN'T ALREADY KNOW ...

▲ Back away from the communications console and turn
   right.

▲ Approach the trio of video kiosks.

▲ Click on each kiosk to view the messages.

Here you learn what the common Atlantean phrase "Until
the Great Reunion" means. These videos speak of high
Atlantean culture and its peaceful pursuit of knowledge; the
cosmic bombardment of the Atlantean home world, prompt-
ing an underground hibernation of the entire race; the deploy-
ment of a colonizing vessel; the founding of Atlantis on an
island continent of a barbaric planet—Earth; the success of the
genetic implantation in human civilizations; the cataclysm
that sank Atlantis; the fate of the outpost ship, and, finally, the
development of time-gate technology.

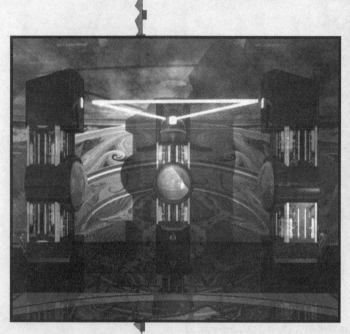

FIGURE 5-15. KIOSK TRIO. THOSE THREE VIDEO KIOSKS OFFER A WEALTH OF HISTORICAL INFORMATION ABOUT THE RISE OF ATLANTIS— AND ITS LITERAL FALL.

▲ After you view all the videos, turn to face the exit door on the opposite wall.

▲ Note carefully the glyph above the door.

FIGURE 5-16. WHO DOES YOUR DOORS? IN ATLANTIS, YOU CAN'T WALK IN OR OUT OF A PLACE WITHOUT BEING OVERPOWERED BY ART. CHECK OUT THE FUNCTIONAL DESIGN ELEMENT ABOVE THIS DOOR.

- ▲ Exit Building Three.

- ▲ Head over to Building Four—the one with the crystal pyramid roof and the semicircular portico with broken columns in front.

- ▲ Enter Building Four.

Building Four

Not even minor structural damage can dampen the beauty of this stunning Atlantean temple. Inside, a pulsating double helix of phosphorescent light hints at the content of the video presentations on the kiosks.

FIGURE 5-17.
BUILDING FOUR

- ▲ Step to the middle of the room and turn right.

- ▲ Approach the video kiosk.

- ▲ Touch the kiosk to trigger the video.

This video discusses the techniques of Atlantean genetic engineering. It also specifies the content of those Gene Pods you've gathered on your journey here: They are actually mod-ified immunization modules for injecting genetic material into biological subjects.

FIGURE 5-18. MISTER GREEN GENES. THIS KIOSK CONFIRMS WHAT YOU ALREADY KNEW—THE GENE PODS ARE INFUSION MODULES CONTAINING THE REFINED GENETIC LEGACY OF THE ATLANTEAN RACE.

▲ Turn around and go to the video kiosk on the opposite side of the room.

▲ Touch the kiosk to trigger another video presentation.

This second kiosk takes a look at the genetic synthesis device that created the Gene Pods. Before the outpost ship—this entire Atlantean complex—can launch off to the home world, all of the Gene Pods must be reattached to the Genetic Device. Then the device itself must be locked to the ship's control panel.

FIGURE 5-19. POD HOLDER. THE OUTPOST SHIP CAN'T MOVE UNTIL THAT DEVICE IS LOCKED ONTO THE CONTROL PANEL WITH ALL GENE PODS IN PLACE.

Before you go, there's something else to see. Each of these outer buildings contains a glyph that's part of a code you need later. In this case, the glyph is more subtly displayed than in the other buildings.

▲ Turn around to face the opposite wall.

▲ Note the glyph design in the center of the floor. (Part of it is cut off from view, but the glyph is the same on all four sides.)

FIGURE 5-20. ON THE FLOOR. NO BIG GLYPHS JUMP OUT AT YOU IN THIS ROOM. SO YOU HAVE TO LOOK CLOSELY.

▲ Exit Building Four.

▲ Take two steps forward.

▲ Turn left and go toward the building at the center of the complex. Let's call it the Central Building. It's cylindrical with a T-shaped entrance, much like an Anasazi kiva.

▲ As you approach, the Guardian pops up on the stairs and says, "I hunger. I need full power." Thanks for sharing, man.

▲ Enter the Central Building.

Central Building: Activating the Elevator

You might expect a building in the very center of a complex to be the most important building. In this case, you would be so right. Lots of important things await you inside the Central Building. But first you have to figure out how to use the elevator.

FIGURE 5-21. CENTRAL BUILDING

▲ Approach the elevator door and turn right.

▲ Step forward to the elevator activation panel.

See the row of building icons across the top row of the panel? Those represent the five buildings in the complex—from left, Buildings One through Four, then the Central Building. If you click on the button under a building icon, it cycles through a series of code glyphs. The object is to cycle to the glyph that you found displayed in the building represented by the icon.

▲ Click on the button under the first building icon (the pyramid of Building One) until you cycle to the glyph that you found by the door inside Building One. (Refer back to Figure 5-8.)

▲ Repeat this process with the next three buttons. For the final solution, see Figure 5-22 below.

▲ Once you've entered the correct code, press the Engage button (the rightmost button in the bottom row) to open the elevator.

Note
You can't enter a code glyph into the elevator activation panel for any location you haven't visited yet. Thus, you must visit all four of the outer buildings before you can enter the elevator.

FIGURE 5-22. WANT A LIFT? ENTER THIS CODE AND PRESS THE ENGAGE BUTTON.

- ▲ Back away from the elevator control panel, turn left, and enter the elevator.

- ▲ Turn around to face the elevator control panel.

- ▲ Only one control button works—the Down button:

Central Building (Lower Level): The Guardian's Crystal

- ▲ After you arrive on the lower level, step forward to exit the elevator. Don't dally.

- ▲ Turn right to see the Guardian in the energy charging station.

FIGURE 5-23. GETTING A CHARGE. EVEN SYNTHETIC SERVANTS NEED A NAP NOW AND THEN. WHILE THE GUARDIAN IS CHARGING, GRAB HIS CRYSTAL AND RUN.

▲ Quickly! Step forward and take the red crystal.

▲ Hurry back into the elevator.

▲ Place the crystal into the slot near the bottom of the elevator control panel.

▲ Click on the Up button.

FIGURE 5-24. GOING UP. PUT THE CRYSTAL IN THE SLOT AND HIT THE UP BUTTON. DON'T FORGET TO REMOVE THE CRYSTAL WHEN YOU REACH THE TOP FLOOR.

Central Building (Upper Level): Activating the Stasis Pod

▲ Just to be safe, SAVE YOUR GAME HERE!

▲ Important: After the elevator stops on the top floor, take the red crystal from its slot! If you don't, the Guardian retrieves it, and you're doomed.

▲ Exit the elevator and step forward to the Atlantean in the stasis pod.

▲ Turn left and proceed to the empty stasis pod.

Want to get rid of the Guardian? Putting him in stasis might be fun. Hearken back to the video on the "star travel stasis pod." To initiate the stasis process, the code panel must be set, and the field generating base must sense the presence of an occupant. And remember that quote: "Where environmental danger is imminent, the pod's code panel may be fully preset, leaving its system in a ready-state." A Guardian on your tail seems like environmental danger to me. But what's the code? There are two ways to find the stasis code:

1. The stasis activation code is entered on the control panel in each stasis pod. Unfortunately, the current pod occupants block your view of parts of their respective panels. If you examine at least two of the pods—one from the left side of the room, one from the right—you can piece together the code. (See Figure 5-25.)

2. Cheat. (See Figure 5-26.)

FIGURE 5-25. PROTOMUMMIES. EXAMINE A COUPLE OF THE
OCCUPIED STASIS PODS TO GET THE STASIS PRESET CODE.

▲ Enter the preset code on the control panel in the empty
stasis pod (see Figure 5-26).

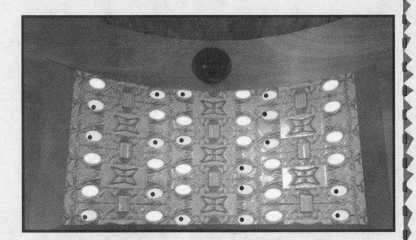

FIGURE 5-26. STASIS POD ACTIVATION CODE

▲ Take two steps back from the stasis chamber. You can see
a hole on the floor.

▲ Put the red crystal in the hole. (You did take the crystal
before you left the elevator, didn't you?)

Warning
After you enter the
code to preset the
stasis pod, don't push
the Engage button
(the big blue button
above the code
buttons). If you do,
you put yourself into
stasis, and your game
is over. But do note
the button's location;
it will be important
later.

FIGURE 5-27.
CRYSTAL BAIT.
THE GUARDIAN'S
LOOKING FOR HIS
CRYSTAL. PUT IT
WHERE YOU WANT
HIM TO GO.

▲ Turn 180 degrees and approach the control panel for the energy beam unit.

▲ Click on the yellow outer triangles until the red sections of all six circles face the center of the polygon (see Figure 5-28).

▲ Click on the red button in the center of the polygon to activate the energy beam unit.

This puzzle is set randomly—that is, it resets differently each time you approach it—so there is no universal solution. It's not too difficult, though. I solved it about 10 times using no particular method (I'm not one of those systematic math guys) and yet it never takes longer than a few minutes.

FIGURE 5-28. ENERGY BEAM CODE. TURN ALL THOSE RED PIE SLICES TO THE MIDDLE, THEN PRESS THE CENTER BUTTON TO ACTIVATE THE "VARIABLE ENERGY BEAM TOOL" (READ: GUN).

▲ After you have completed the Energy Beam Code puzzle, SAVE YOUR GAME HERE!

▲ Step back from the solved Energy Beam Code puzzle to automatically enter the energy beam unit. Once inside the unit, note that your cursor is now a targeting reticule.

Get ready! At this point, the Guardian materializes in front of you. He grabs the crystal you planted on the floor of the stasis pod. And he's standing right in your gunsights. You cannot terminate him with energy beam blasts—but you can knock him around a bit.

▲ Quickly! Shoot the Guardian until he backs into the stasis pod.

▲ Quickly! Shoot the pod's Engage button—the big button at the top of the control panel.

Note
This was designed to be a "trap" for the Doom-style twitch gamers. You can't kill the Guardian by simply shooting him. You have to outsmart him by trapping him in the stasis pod.

Tip
Shoot the Guardian in the chest to push him back. If you shoot him anywhere else, he'll be unaffected.

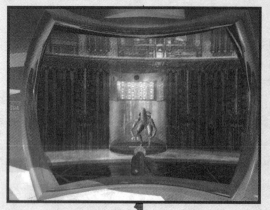

FIGURE 5-29. THE BIG SLEEP. KNOCK THE GUARDIAN INTO THE POD WITH ENERGY BLASTS, THEN SHOOT THE BIG BUTTON ON THE CONTROL PANEL TO PUT HIM INTO TEMPORARY STASIS.

▲ Turn right to exit the energy beam unit.

▲ SAVE YOUR GAME HERE!

▲ Turn left and step forward to the Guardian in the stasis pod.

▲ Turn left and proceed through the doors to the Control Room. (The Guardian's appearance unlocked these doors.)

Central Building (Upper Level): Control Room/Escape Pod

▲ Just inside the doors, turn right and approach the Genetic Device.

▲ Click on the device to open it. You see the Atlantis Gene Pod and three empty slots.

▲ Open your Gene Pod inventory (Control + G or ⌘ + G in Macontosh version) and click on any of the pods. They automatically transfer to the Genetic Device.

220

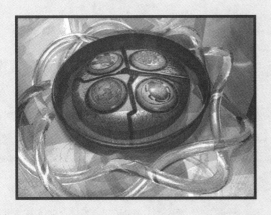

FIGURE 5-30.
GENETIC DEVICE.
GO TO THAT POD
HOLDER ON THE
WALL AND FILL IT
WITH YOUR
ACCUMULATED
GENE PODS.

▲ Take the Genetic Device.

▲ Optional: You can turn around, enter the transportal room, and listen to the professor's advice. But it's just a waste of time.

▲ Facing the Genetic Device, turn left and go to launch control panel at the other end of the room.

▲ In the close-up, click on the button (center of panel) to prepare the entire complex for launch. This also activates the escape pod, back in the elevator.

▲ SAVE YOUR GAME HERE!

▲ Place the Genetic Device in the launch control panel.

▲ Run! You have two minutes until launch.

▲ Quickly! Hurry to the elevator and press the Escape Pod button on the elevator control panel.

FIGURE 5-31.
LAUNCH AND ESCAPE.

DEPRESS THE LAUNCH CONTROL BUTTON, PLACE THE
GENETIC DEVICE ON THE PANEL, AND RUN LIKE HELL FOR THE
ELEVATOR. IF YOU MAKE IT BEFORE LAUNCH, HIT THAT ESCAPE
POD BUTTON (JUST ABOVE THE CRYSTAL SLOT).

Timelapse Game Endings

I won't spoil the fun by showing screen shots from the ending.
But you should know that there are six possible Timelapse
endings. The following are the scenarios for all six.

Outcome 1

The Atlantis outpost ship self-destructs with you aboard. The
self-destruct timer starts if you attempt to leave the control
room with the Genetic Device. Note that the escape pod will
not launch if it detects the Genetic Device. Note also that you
·can override the self-destruct sequence by placing the Genetic
Device in the launch control panel. If you still have it—you
didn't give it to the professor, did you? If you did, the self-
destruct timer will be started. Not a good thing. This activates
the 60-second launch sequence.

Outcome 2

The Atlantis outpost ship launches for a return to the Atlantean home world. You remain aboard the huge ship as it blasts off through the Earth's atmosphere and journeys home. The launch sequence begins when you load the Genetic Device into the launch control panel.

Outcome 3

The Atlantis outpost ship launches for the Atlantean home world. But before the launch sequence finishes, you hustle to the elevator and launch the escape pod. If you escape, you view the magnificent launch from a distance.

Outcome 4

Stasis! You entered the stasis pod, set the activation code—and then pushed the Engage button while standing in the pod. The Guardian mocks you. "Game over man!"

Outcome 5

You are trapped on Atlantis. You can activate neither the self-destruct nor the launch sequences because you destroyed the Gene Pods by giving them to the professor in the transportal. Hey, have a good life! Maybe those frozen Atlanteans know some good card games.

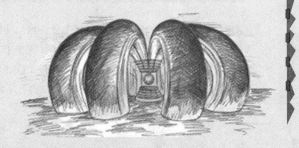

Outcome 6

The Guardian tosses you into the "timeless dimension" of the transportal. Now you'd better hope Professor Nichols knows a few card games. This outcome happens if any of the following occur:

▲ You take the crystal from the Guardian at the charging station and dally getting into the elevator.

▲ You leave the crystal in the elevator after riding up to the top level.

▲ You leave the crystal in the elevator and enter the middle level.

▲ You hang out too long anywhere upstairs with the crystal. The Guardian eventually becomes fully charged and gets you.

▲ You can't force the Guardian into the stasis pod.

FIGURE 5-32. GOOD-BYE EARTH, HELLO HOME WORLD.
GUESS YOU DIDN'T GET TO THE ESCAPE POD ON TIME.
IT'S OK, THOUGH. I HEAR THE HOME WORLD HAS A LOT OF
GREAT MICROBREWERIES. AND MAYBE TIMELAPSE II
WILL GET YOU BACK HOME.

PART THREE

Interview with the
Timelapse Team

ES, YOUR FIRST IMPRESSION is correct—*Timelapse* was inspired by *Myst*. But no doubt your second impression was the same as mine: This game takes the genre established by *Myst* to fabulous new heights. Traversing the *Timelapse* universe, you can't help but admire the integrity of the product, the remarkable attention to detail in all phases of design—art and animation, music and sound, puzzle design and game play, writing and story. Clearly, *Timelapse* was rendered by loving hands.

So when I talked to the design team shortly before the game's release, I wasn't surprised to learn that *Timelapse* was indeed a labor of love. Producer and Lead Designer Lori Nichols revealed that "[designing this game] was definitely a passion for everyone involved." The original concept arose from Nichols' own interest in archaeology and her admiration for *Myst*. In this interview, Nichols and other *Timelapse* team members speak of the game's genesis and development. The final product, two years in the making, speaks quite eloquently for itself.

I conducted this interview via speakerphone in late August of 1996, just a couple of weeks before *Timelapse* was released to the manufacturer for mass reproduction. The GTE Entertainment team—Tim Bank, Ed Deren, Lori Nichols, and Mike Yuen—spoke from an office in their headquarters at Carlsbad, California. The session, as you'll see, was lively and full of good humor.

CLOCKWISE FROM THE UPPER LEFT: FRANCISCO VILLASEÑOR, LORI NICHOLS, SAL PARASCANDOLO, MIKE YUEN, ED DEREN, TIM BANK.

Introduction

RICK BARBA: Let's go around the room first. Introduce yourself and tell us your role on the *Timelapse* project.

MIKE YUEN: Hello, I'm Mike Yuen, Product Marketing Manager for *Timelapse*. I joined GTE Entertainment last May when the game was in concept stage, so I've been with the project from the beginning. I had a little of design input into the game (the Anasazi paw print puzzle was mine), however, my focus was primarily on reviewing and editing the writing. I also did a lot of the logic/continuity testing of the story and puzzles.

RB: An important role in this game, I would think.

MIKE YUEN: Yeah, one thing we wanted to achieve in *Timelapse* was to make the story and puzzles as "tight" as possible. Next, what we did was ground things in fact and then take creative license to make this entertaining. After all, this is a game and not a reference title.

ED DEREN: Hi, I'm Ed Deren. I've been at GTE Entertainment for about three years. Lori Nichols had the original idea of doing an adventure game based on ancient civilizations. And from there, we sat down together and came up with some of the original scenarios for the game. I was responsible for the game design for Egypt. I did the art direction and some of the illustration for Egypt, as well. I also oversaw a large portion of the audio design for the entire game. My background is in animation and background painting.

LORI NICHOLS: My name is Lori Nichols. I'm the Producer and Lead Designer of four of the worlds (Easter Island, Anasazi, Maya, and Atlantis) in *Timelapse*. I directed the live-action shoot and also art directed the project along with Ed Deren and Alan Anders. I've been with GTE Entertainment for five years. In addition, I'm the Director of Creative Services and company Art Director. My background is in special effects and broadcast graphics.

RB: It's interesting that you came out of Creative Services into game design. Is it fluid that way at GTE Entertainment? Can people from other departments move into Product Development?

LORI NICHOLS: Sure, if you're extremely motivated and willing to do your original job in addition to that. [Laughs.] I approached Dick Robinson, the President and CEO, and said I'd be willing to continue doing my full-time job, and also take this project on. It's been a real team effort. Everyone on the team has worked incredible hours the last couple of years—weekends, nights—to make *Timelapse* happen. Dick was also very supportive of the project, which helped keep things moving along smoothly.

RB: I think that's a key part of the making of *Timelapse* story. It's clearly a labor of love for you guys.

LORI NICHOLS: Yes, that's certainly true. My personal interest in archaeology was one of the driving forces behind the basic design of the game—which worlds you visit, how they're linked, the lost city of Atlantis, etc. It's interesting to note that the concept of Atlantis being linked to other ancient civilizations has been around for quite a long time. The special " X-factor" we threw in was the alien element.

TIM BANK: Hi, I'm Tim Bank. I'm a Software Engineer. I've been here at GTE Entertainment for about three years now. I'm primarily responsible for prototyping all the puzzles and working out a lot of the continuity and technical aspects of *Timelapse*.

Game Concept

RB: OK, now that we're all acquainted, let's talk more about the original concept. Where did it come from? What inspired it?

LORI NICHOLS: Well, it probably comes as no surprise that it started with *Myst*. It combined puzzles, graphics, and story in a style that I had never seen before. So we started talking about how we could improve it. What would it take to create a game like *Myst*, only better? As I mentioned before, I've always been fascinated with archaeology. In particular, the ancient Egyptians, Mayans, and the Anasazi. I'm also a real sci-fi buff, which inspired the Atlantis/alien aspect to the game.

So Ed and I sat down and asked, "Can we design a graphical adventure around ancient civilizations, their linkage, Atlantis, and aliens?" We threw around some initial ideas and put together a game prototype—Ed designed a portion of Egypt, which Tim then programmed. Next, we presented the prototype to the PRC (Product Review Committee). The PRC is made up of members from each of the key functional departments within the company (Product Development, Sales, Marketing, etc.). As a team this group decides whether or not a prototype gets the OK to become a full game. *Timelapse* was approved.

MIKE YUEN: We also did a lot of consumer focus group testing early on with graphical adventure gamers. We tested the basic concept of *Timelapse* to see if people would be interested in a game about ancient civilizations, Atlantis, time travel, etc. This allowed us to fine tune and tweak the concept before starting into full game production. We also asked gamers what they liked/disliked about games like *Myst* and what they would do to improve them. For example, the fact that we have an "instant" camera feature in *Timelapse* is a direct result of focus group testers saying that they would have liked something like this in *Myst*. All of the feedback we received was invaluable in helping to shape the game based on what the consumer/market wanted.

LORI NICHOLS: After approval of the prototype, we started in on the actual game development. It was very much a team effort. Everybody had their say, and we really tried to encourage this kind of feedback. Ed and I designed puzzles for each of our respective worlds, and everybody then took a stab at analyzing them and chopping them up. Mike, in particular, really hammered out the logical aspects of the puzzles. A lot of the credit for implementation goes to people like Tim and Francisco Villaseñor, people who analyzed the elements and made sure they actually played well.

RB: By the way, how long ago did you present the concept to the PRC? How long has *Timelapse* been in the making?

LORI NICHOLS: Ed and I have been at it from the very beginning, going back two-and-a-half years. The actual concept itself was presented more than two years ago. There was a six month prototype phase where we examined what it would take technically to create this game. We wanted to ray trace and render the entire game on high-end SGIs [Silicon Graphics workstations]. That hadn't been done before at 640-by-480 resolution. We also wanted to incorporate 360-degree panoramic turns to facilitate better navigation. The actual development of the game took about 18 to 20 months to complete.

The Story

RB: Once you settled on the original concept, what was the next step? How did you develop the story and script?

LORI NICHOLS: We hired a writer, Dick Moran, and brought him down for brainstorming sessions with the core team, which included the four of us here, plus Francisco Villaseñor [Production Manager], Sal Parascandolo [Assistant Producer], and Alan Anders [Lead 3D Animator]. As always, everybody put in their two cents worth. After many meetings, impromptu hallway discussions, and constantly going over all of the logical points, we finally generated the game's story (which is revealed through the professor's journal and various video segments in the game). We knew that a good story was critical and we wanted everything to fall into place and make "sense."

Mike Yuen: The goal was to create a story based on real civilizations. I think people feel strongly connected to the past and by adding the Atlantis/alien element, this makes for compelling story telling.

RB: So the story in *Timelapse* evolved as the result of a collaborative effort?

LORI NICHOLS: Yes, very much so. We did a lot of research into the various elements of the cultures—for example, the way the Egyptians counted, or the fact that the Mayans practiced human sacrifice, or the Egyptians had complex mechanisms for irrigation. We wanted to focus on what really made "sense" in each of the worlds. We also wanted the puzzles to be as "natural" and seamlessly integrated into the story and worlds as possible.

Puzzle Design

RB: I think one of the most interesting aspects of the game is the fact that the various worlds and their puzzles are actually integrated together.

MIKE YUEN: Yeah, what's neat about *Timelapse* is that you may have to solve a puzzle that requires you to learn the actual Egyptian counting system and you might not even realize this is in fact what you just did.

ED DEREN: I worked on the irrigation puzzle at the boat dock in Egypt, where you have to open the gate by using the weight of water and pulleys and ropes. I wanted the mechanism to look like it was part of the world, but at the same time make it pretty intricate. I love this kind of puzzle, where you have to walk around the mechanism, play with things, figure out all of the relationships between various components—a basket, a well bucket, water in the trough, levers.

RB: It's another example of a puzzle that's indigenous to the world, that isn't just a puzzle for the sake of having a puzzle.

MIKE YUEN: One of the things we tried to do was vary the type of puzzles in each of the worlds. For example, they're not all logic based, or based on mathematics. Some are mechanical in nature like the Egyptian irrigation system Ed just described, others are based on sound, some are spatial while others are skill games. We wanted a wide variety of puzzles for appeal to a broad audience of gamers out there.

RB: Yeah, well, Einstein couldn't have solved the Crystal Pyramid Puzzle [in the Mayan Lizard Temple].

[General laughter.]

LORI NICHOLS: Everybody who play tested that puzzle said, "This thing's impossible!" So we put in the page from the codex book with the solution nearby on the floor. Use that in concert with the journal, and the puzzle isn't as tough as it seems.

Up-front testing was a really critical component in our puzzle design process. Tim's prototypes were very valuable to this project. We were able to ask people, "Is this too hard? Too easy? Is it fun?" We then took this feedback and incorporated it into the game's final puzzles.

TIM BANK: It was good to get a sense of how the game felt before going into full production. I could actually take something, sketch it down on a piece of paper, scan it in, then take it into Director and make a puzzle prototype out of it. Then I'd e-mail that to a few people for comments. I'd get their thoughts back and then tweak the puzzle some more, make it harder or easier, then pass it on to the animators. By then, they'd know all of the puzzle components. So before it was integrated we'd already have a really good idea about how the puzzle worked and played.

LORI NICHOLS: We also paid a lot of attention to the balance of the puzzles. You can't always control the order that people solve the puzzles, but we generally started each world with something easy—for example, a physical puzzle like finding the log to cross the chasm in the Anasazi world, or finding the amulet in the Mayan world. We wanted a nice balance of hard and easy puzzles, and a good mix of puzzle types. This is a family game too. I think younger kids might not be able to solve all of the puzzles, but you could play the game with them—play as a family.

RB: I think one of the most interesting aspects of the *Timelapse* development story—the fact that you, Lori, came up with the original concept and designed the game. Aside from Sierra, where Roberta Williams [designer of the *King's Quest* series and the recent *Phantasmagoria*] and Jane Jensen [designer of the *Gabriel Knight* mysteries] are design stars, there are almost no female designers in this industry. And that's a shame. I think *Timelapse* will join the ranks of *Myst* as a title that opens a lot of eyes to the fact that you don't have to target a male audience and blow up stuff to have a successful product.

LORI NICHOLS: Well, we did throw in a few things for the "boys." [Laughs.] You get to stab a crocodile. You get to hack at vines with a machete, and shoot a bow-and-arrow.

RB: True. I just completed the part of the game where you blast the Guardian back into the stasis chamber in Atlantis. I'm feeling more like a man now. [General laughter.]

LORI NICHOLS: Our hope is to entice the DOOM-style twitch gamers into thinking they have to kill the Guardian, which you can't do. [Laughter.] You have to outsmart the Guardian. After all this is a puzzle-based adventure game!

The Journal

RB: Who wrote the professor's journal for the game?

LORI NICHOLS: The journal was a collaborative effort between Dick Moran, Sal Parascandolo, Mike Yuen, and myself. Mike also edited it. Dick Moran would take a first pass. Then Sal and I would rework the passages based on the game play, and Mike would copyedit them. A big part of it was just cross-checking the logic. One of the challenges was to write the journal from the professor's point of view in the order that he traveled through the worlds. He starts at Easter Island, then goes to Egypt, Maya, Anasazi, and finally Atlantis. In Atlantis, just before he is trapped by the Guardian, he is able to send his journal back through the time gate to Easter Island. Since the player doesn't have to go in this same order [for three of the worlds] we had to ensure that the journal would still make sense.

We purposely tried to include a lot of facts from our research in the journal. We wanted to deepen the game experience by including elements that were actual and true. Of course, we took creative license to tweak them where we needed to, to keep things fun. Like Mike said earlier, this is a game. Overall, a tremendous amount of effort went into the development of the journal.

The Worlds

RB: I was impressed by the distinct character of the individual worlds. For example, Egypt. How did that world evolve?

ED DEREN: I've always been fascinated with ancient Egypt. I thought it was an absolutely gorgeous world. As an artist, I started as a metalsmith and a sculptor. So I viewed the digital creation of *Timelapse*'s Egyptian world from a visual and physical perspective.

We thought it was also important to use the mythology and religious figures from the particular cultures in *Timelapse*. In Egypt, we came up with eight of the main gods of that culture and tried to weave them into the story and game play. Also, our world is based on actual archaeological structures—the samples of architecture you see in the game may actually span a couple of thousand of years, but they're authentic.

LORI NICHOLS: In *Timelapse*, you might find something from Tutankhamun's tomb and something from Ramses' tomb. They're separated by a thousand years, but they're based on authentic Egyptian artifacts. Again, we tried to be as faithful to the cultures as possible.

We also tried to add a lot of indigenous life to the worlds—lizards, birds, snakes, cats, monkeys—via animations. We wanted to immerse the player into the worlds. For example, we added blowing grass, flying birds, and moving water; in total, there are over 500 animations in *Timelapse*.

ED DEREN: We learned from our focus group testing that one of the big complaints among players of *Myst* was that, "The worlds seemed so devoid of life."

LORI NICHOLS: Lance Hutto and Craig Deeley did a great job with the 2D animation. Alan Anders was our Lead 3D Animator, and he was instrumental in creating the 3D graphics along with Susan Hayden, Mark Macy, and Ed Yaffa. An example of how we would design a world is I'd meet with the 3D artist and we'd review the puzzles I designed and discuss their implementation into a 3D world. Then, we'd do rough sketches and agree on a general overall direction—the lighting, the time of day, the cultural elements, etc.

One of the challenges we faced was how to set this game outside [in addition to being inside]. Creating realistic-looking outside worlds in 3D is incredibly difficult. You have very large wireframe files to work with which are tough to render, especially if you're ray tracing like we did in *Timelapse*. Basically, ray tracing is a mathematical equation of light. It calculates how light actually strikes an object and causes reflection and shadows. We had some frames that took six to eight hours to render! Especially shots with foliage in them. Most of the objects are 3D-modeled. The Anasazi world, in particular, was very challenging to create since it existed almost entirely outside. Susan [Hayden] did a fantastic job recreating the American Southwest. The environments in each of the worlds except Atlantis, of course, are based on the true terrain of each location. We did extensive research on the types of plants, animals, and terrain. It's all indigenous. There were nine SGIs crunching around the clock, 24 hours a day, seven days a week.

MIKE YUEN: We actually had press who came to visit GTE Entertainment to preview the game and when we showed them some of the images they looked so real to them that they would ask, "If the wind's blowing, why aren't those branches moving?"

TIM BANK: Or they'd come back in an hour and wonder why the shadows haven't moved. [Laughter.]

LORI NICHOLS: In fact, that's an element we'll definitely look at for the next project, the element of time. How things change over time.

ED DEREN: One of my favorite "criticisms" of the game came from a guy who looked at *Timelapse* and said, "So what? You digitized a bunch of photographs. What's the big deal?" [General laughter.] I thought that was just the most wonderful compliment we could get.

MIKE YUEN: Some people even thought we had a reference title because the images looked so real.

By the way, I wanted to mention that you will find a lot of the artists' names on the various objects at the professor's campsite on Easter Island. For example, you'll see Villaseñor Matches.

RB: I also noticed some of your names in the journal.

LORI NICHOLS: [Laughs.] To be honest, my son's name is Alexander Nichols, and it was supposed to be just a placeholder. But our PR department leaked the name, and we thought we shouldn't be changing things since the name seemed to "work." Anyway, he's too young to sue us. [Laughter.] We had fun with people's names in the journal. Remember the Collins Gas Lantern? Well, Jeanne Collins is GTE Entertainment's Testing Manager, so we wanted to pay her a tribute.

RB: How did you come up with your visual concept for Atlantis?

LORI NICHOLS: I researched Atlantis and found Plato's description of what he believed it to be. I was trying to visualize what a futuristic world built in the past would look like. I have a real affinity for classic art deco shapes so I wanted to incorporate this aspect into the world's design. I started with a top-view layout, with some simple sketches of the buildings I wanted to see. They had to be reminiscent of ancient cultures, but be built with high-tech modern materials. Some of the Atlantean buildings resemble Egyptian or Mayan architecture, and the central building has a cylindrical kiva-like shape with a T-shaped doorway, which is an Anasazi symbol. We roughly based our concept of Atlantis on the island of Thera. The idea was to create a site that was the nucleus of civilization. Originally, we planned a bigger Atlantis. But we decided we'd really go to town with Atlantis in *Timelapse II*. Hogie McMurtry designed the Atlantean alphabet and also did some concept sketches.

The Actors

RB: Where'd you get your actors?

LORI NICHOLS: Most of them are from Los Angeles or San Diego. We went to local casting agencies to cast the characters. John Paval played the professor. The actors appear in short video sequences designed to give the player game backstory.

Sound and Audio

RB: I was impressed with the quality of the sound and music in the game, too. Creating a totally immersive atmosphere is so important in this genre of game....

ED DEREN: Dom Widiez put together the sound in the movies, the openings, and the time gates. I sat down and scripted out where all of the sounds went. We literally had hundreds and hundreds of sounds. Sal Parascandolo came up with a lot of the internal music for the different worlds, as well as Scott Scheinbaum from CyberFlix. He did a wonderful job.

LORI NICHOLS: Sal's actually at home as we speak working on audio. He's been critical to the success of *Timelapse*. We also bought the rights to one of the songs, "Invoking the Hawk's Spirit" by The Mesa Music Consort, published by Talking Taco Recordings. It's the song we use in the Anasazi world. It's a beautiful piece written by Native Americans. It really fit the spirit of what we wanted in the Anasazi world. We also used sound clips from the Ethnic Loops Audio Library, so many of the sounds are actually ethnic instruments looped with other music. Again, we tried to stay true to each culture, even in our sounds and music. Except for Atlantis, of course. [Laughs.]

Timelapse II

RB: So, will there be a *Timelapse II,* a sequel?

LORI NICHOLS: We're putting together our proposal now.

MIKE YUEN: We're currently looking at a number of ideas for a sequel. For example, one potential concept comes from the game ending in *Timelapse* where you're stuck on the colony outpost ship as it blasts off for the alien home world. That's one contender, setting *Timelapse II* on the alien home planet. We're looking at how we can tie the home world to some of the unexplained phenomena here on Earth like the Bermuda Triangle. I think that could be pretty cool.

LORI NICHOLS: The alien home world might be a blend of ancient cultures, as well. There are some interesting ones that we just couldn't incorporate into *Timelapse*— the Great Zimbabwe, the Incas, Angkor Wat—due to time constraints to get the game done. There are a lot of fascinating ancient cultures that are very mysterious. So we're thinking about tying some of these into the sequel to maintain the theme established with *Timelapse*.

RB: I would hate to see that element go away, the real archaeological basis for the worlds.

LORI NICHOLS: Exactly. So in *Timelapse II* maybe you start on Earth, and you're investigating the Incas or the Bermuda Triangle, and you discover another time gate that ties you back to the alien home world. I agree the archaeological basis is a real strength of the game, and we plan to keep that element in any sequels we do. Plus, archaeology really enthralls me anyway.

RB: You might as well do what enthralls you.

LORI NICHOLS: [Laughs.] It's the only way to go! We'd also like to use the next level of technology. I don't think we'll go to real-time game play because the graphics quality is still not there yet. With *Timelapse* we wanted to make an incredibly beautiful game that had great game play. That will be our goal in any sequel, too. By this Christmas, we'll see where the technology is with 3D accelerator cards and chips, QuickTime VR, etc., and see what makes sense.

MIKE YUEN: Another thing for the sequel that we'd like to do is to add some type of online component to it, whether it's a multiplayer option or something that's networked—which is very tough to do by the very nature of an adventure game. Nevertheless, we're trying to come up with some creative and innovative ways to do this. For example, maybe you need to have someone else doing something at the same time as you elsewhere in the game world. This implies both a multiplayer and networked aspect to the game.

Until the Great Reunion

RB: Before we sign off, is there anything else you want to say to your fans out there reading this interview now?

LORI NICHOLS: It's been a privilege working with such talented software engineers as Danny Aijala, Bill Appleton, Tim Bank, Curtis Jablonski, and Ian McClean. I also want to stress again what a true team effort *Timelapse* was. Everybody on the team contributed. It was just an incredible group to work with. And we're going to do everything we can to stay together and make another one.

MIKE YUEN: Until the Great Reunion!

Prima
The World Leader in

Sid Meier's Civilization® II
The Official Strategy Guide

Leave your everlasting mark on civilization! Imagine what the world would be like if you could personally sculpt history from the dawn of time. Would you build the Roman Empire? Construct the Great Wall of China? Discover a cure for cancer? However you choose to rewrite history, don't make a single decision without consulting this guide.

$19.95
ISBN 1-7615-0106-1
By David Ellis

Duke Nukem 3D™
Unauthorized Game Secrets

You need more than pipebombs and true grit to make it out of L.A. alive and save the earth. What you need are the secrets in this guide. Inside you'll find, detailed maps for every mission, the locations of all secret areas, atom-smashing combat tactics, game-busting cheat codes, and much more.

$14.99
ISBN 0-7615-0783-3
By Michael van Mantgem and Kip Ward

WarCraft™ II
Beyond the Dark Portal
Official Secrets & Solutions

Only a fool would go wading through the fetid swamps of the Orcish homeland unprepared. Before you venture beyond the Dark Portal and into the twisted terrain of 24 new missions, you'd better have this guide. With this book's brutal strategies, you'll fit right in.

$14.99
ISBN 0-7615-0787-6
By Mark Walker

WarCraft™ II
Tides of Darkness
The Official Strategy Guide

No matter which side they choose, this guide will keep gamers on the victorious end of the pounding, pillaging, and plundering! From Zeppelins to Gryphon Riders, it's easy to build impermeable defenses and launch brutal assaults when you've got this book!

$19.95
ISBN 0-7615-0188-6
By Ed Dille

Prima Publishing
PO Box 629000 • El Dorado Hills, CA 95762
To Order Call 1•800•531•2343

Secrets of the Games® is a registered trademark of Prima Publishing, a division of Prima Communications, Inc.

Publishing
Electronic Entertainment Books!

Ultimate Mortal Kombat™ 3
Official Arcade Secrets

The ultimate showdown awaits, and this guide is your ultimate source of UMK3 knowledge! It reveals ALL ultimate kombat kodes and hidden kontenders, blow-by-blow details to master all 22 kombatants, more than 300 killer kombos that will allow you to crush the opposition, and the lowdown on playing UMK3 on the Sega Saturn.

$9.99
ISBN 0-7615-0586-5
By Chris Rice and Simon Hill

Hexen™
The Official Strategy Guide

Enter the ultimate sword and sorcery battlefest that is Hexen! Destroy the Serpent Rider, and restore order to the Chronos dimension before it's too late! Whether players do battle as the mage, cleric, and fighter, this guide has what they need to complete their mission!

$19.95
ISBN 1-7615-0388-9
By Joe Bell Grant

Myst™
The Official Strategy Guide, Revised and Expanded Edition

In this #1 bestselling, ultimate, authoritative source for answers and information about Myst Island and the Ages of Myst, gamers will find a complete fictionalized walkthrough of Myst, detailed information about the many puzzles, screen images of the most important locations, and much more!

$19.95
ISBN 0-7615-0102-9
By Rick Barba and Rusel DeMaria

Prima's Sony PlayStation™ Game Secrets
The Unauthorized Edition Vol. 2

The Sony PlayStation is an electronic adrenaline rush of state-of-the-art gameplay, and this book is your definitive guide to all the pulse-pounding action. Whether you're into reflex-testing arcade games, martial arts mayhem, sports, war games, or role-playing, this compendium is packed with inside information you won't find anywhere else.

$12.99
ISBN 0-7615-0515-6
By Prima Creative Services, Vince Matthews, and Douglas R. Brumley

PRIMA'S
SECRETS
OF THE GAMES

clude your VISA or Mastercard number, expiration date, and your name and address. Please add $4.00 shipping and handling for the first book, ($1.00 for each additional ook) in the U.S. (California residents add 7.25% sales tax, Tennessee residents add 8.25% sales tax, Maryland residents add 5% sales tax, Indiana residents add 5% sales x). Allow 2-3 weeks for delivery. Canadian orders please add $6.00 shipping and handling ($1.00 for each additional book) and 7% GST. U.S. funds only, please.

ima's Secrets of the Games® series is distributed in the UK and EEC by Boxtree Ltd. Look for Prima books at your local bookshop, or order directly through tlehampton Book Services: Tel. 44 (0) 1903 732596 Fax 44 (0) 1903 730914 *Access, Visa and Mastercard accepted.*

to order, call prima at
1-800-531-2343

Computer Game Books

1942: The Pacific Air War—The Official Strategy Guide	$19.95
The 11th Hour: The Official Strategy Guide	$19.95
The 7th Guest: The Official Strategy Guide	$19.95
Aces Over Europe: The Official Strategy Guide	$19.95
Across the Rhine: The Official Strategy Guide	$19.95
Alone in the Dark 3: The Official Strategy Guide	$19.95
Armored Fist: The Official Strategy Guide	$19.95
Ascendancy: The Official Strategy Guide	$19.95
Buried in Time: The Journeyman Project 2—The Official Strategy Guide	$19.95
CD-ROM Games Secrets, Volume 1	$19.95
CD-ROM Games Secrets, Volume 2	$19.99
CD-ROM Classics	$19.99
Caesar II: The Official Strategy Guide	$19.95
Celtic Tales: Balor of the Evil Eye—The Official Strategy Guide	$19.95
Cyberia: The Official Strategy Guide	$19.95
Cyberia2: The Official Strategy Guide	$19.99
Dark Seed II: The Official Strategy Guide	$19.95
Descent: The Official Strategy Guide	$19.95
Descent II: The Official Strategy Guide	$19.99
DOOM Battlebook	$19.95
DOOM II: The Official Strategy Guide	$19.95
Dragon Lore: The Official Strategy Guide	$19.95
Dungeon Master II: The Legend of Skullkeep—The Official Strategy Guide	$19.95
Fleet Defender: The Official Strategy Guide	$19.95
Frankenstein: Through the Eyes of the Monster—The Official Strategy Guide	$19.95
Front Page Sports Football Pro '95: The Official Playbook	$19.95
Fury3: The Official Strategy Guide	$19.95
Hell: A Cyberpunk Thriller—The Official Strategy Guide	$19.95
Heretic: The Official Strategy Guide	$19.95
I Have No Mouth, and I Must Scream: The Official Strategy Guide	$19.95
In The 1st Degree: The Official Strategy Guide	$19.95
Kingdom: The Far Reaches—The Official Strategy Guide	$14.95
King's Quest VII: The Unauthorized Strategy Guide	$19.95
The Legend of Kyrandia: The Official Strategy Guide	$19.95
Lords of Midnight: The Official Strategy Guide	$19.95
Machiavelli the Prince: Official Secrets & Solutions	$12.95
Marathon: The Official Strategy Guide	$19.95
Master of Orion: The Official Strategy Guide	$19.95
Master of Magic: The Official Strategy Guide	$19.95
MechWarrior 2: The Official Strategy Guide	$19.95
Microsoft Arcade: The Official Strategy Guide	$12.95
Microsoft Flight Simulator 5.1: The Official Strategy Guide	$19.95
Microsoft Golf: The Official Strategy Guide	$19.95
Microsoft Space Simulator: The Official Strategy Guide	$19.95
Might and Magic Compendium: The Authorized Strategy Guide for Games I, II, III, and IV	$19.95
Mission Critical: The Official Strategy Guide	$19.95
Myst: The Official Strategy Guide	$19.95
Online Games: In-Depth Strategies and Secrets	$19.95
Oregon Trail II: The Official Strategy Guide	$19.95
Panzer General: The Official Strategy Guide	$19.95
Perfect General II: The Official Strategy Guide	$19.95
Prince of Persia: The Official Strategy Guide	$19.95
Prisoner of Ice: The Official Strategy Guide	$19.95
The Residents: Bad Day on the Midway— The Official Strategy Guide	$19.95
Return to Zork Adventurer's Guide	$14.95
Ripper: The Official Strategy Guide	$19.99

Romance of the Three Kingdoms IV: Wall of Fire—The Official Strategy Guide	$19.95
Shannara: The Official Strategy Guide	$19.95
Sid Meier's Civilization, or Rome on 640K a Day	$19.95
Sid Meier's Civilization II: The Official Strategy Guide	$19.99
Sid Meier's Colonization: The Official Strategy Guide	$19.95
SimCity 2000: Power, Politics, and Planning	$19.95
SimEarth: The Official Strategy Guide	$19.95
SimFarm Almanac: The Official Guide to SimFarm	$19.95
SimLife: The Official Strategy Guide	$19.95
SimTower: The Official Strategy Guide	$19.95
Stonekeep: The Official Strategy Guide	$19.95
SubWar 2050: The Official Strategy Guide	$19.95
Terry Pratchett's Discworld: The Official Strategy Guide	$19.95
Thunderscape: The Official Strategy Guide	$19.95
TIE Fighter Collector's CD-ROM: The Official Strategy Guide	$19.99
Under a Killing Moon: The Official Strategy Guide	$19.95
WarCraft: Orcs & Humans Official Secrets & Solutions	$9.95
WarCraft II: Tides of Darkness—The Official Strategy Guide	$19.99
Warlords II Deluxe: The Official Strategy Guide	$19.95
Werewolf Vs. Commanche: The Official Strategy Guide	$19.95
Wing Commander I, II, and III: The Ultimate Strategy Guide	$19.95
X-COM Terror From The Deep: The Official Strategy Guide	$19.95
X-COM UFO Defense: The Official Strategy Guide	$19.95
X-Wing Collector's CD-ROM: The Official Strategy Guide	$19.95

Video Game Books

3DO Game Guide	$16.95
Battle Arena Toshinden Game Secrets: The Unauthorized Edition	$12.95
Behind the Scenes at Sega: The Making of a Video Game	$14.95
Breath of Fire Authorized Game Secrets	$14.95
Breath of Fire II Authorized Game Secrets	$14.95
Complete Final Fantasy III Forbidden Game Secrets	$14.95
Donkey Kong Country Game Secrets the Unauthorized Edition	$9.95
Donkey Kong Country 2—Diddy's Kong Quest Unauthorized Game Secrets	$12.99
EA SPORTS Official Power Play Guide	$12.95
Earthworm Jim Official Game Secrets	$12.95
Earthworm Jim 2 Official Game Secrets	$14.95
GEX: The Official Power Play Guide	$14.95
Killer Instinct Game Secrets: The Unauthorized Edition	$9.95
Killer Instinct 2 Unauthorized Arcade Secrets	$12.99
The Legend of Zelda: A Link to the Past—Game Secrets	$12.95
Lord of the Rings Official Game Secrets	$12.95
Maximum Carnage Official Game Secrets	$9.95
Mortal Kombat II Official Power Play Guide	$9.95
Mortal Kombat 3 Official Arcade Secrets	$9.95
Mortal Kombat 3 Official Power Play Guide	$9.95
NBA JAM: The Official Power Play Guide	$12.95
Ogre Battle: The March of the Black Queen—The Official Power Play Guide	$14.95
Parent's Guide to Video Games	$12.95
PlayStation Game Secrets: The Unauthorized Edition, Vol. 1	$12.99
Secret of Evermore: Authorized Power Play Guide	$12.95
Secret of Mana Official Game Secrets	$14.95
Street Fighter Alpha—Warriors' Dreams Unauthorized Game Secrets	$12.99
Ultimate Mortal Kombat 3 Official Arcade Secrets	$9.99
Urban Strike Official Power Play Guide, with Desert Strike & Jungle Strike	$12.95

To Order Books

Please send me the following items:

Quantity	Title	Unit Price	Total
_____	_____	$ _____	$ _____
_____	_____	$ _____	$ _____
_____	_____	$ _____	$ _____
_____	_____	$ _____	$ _____
_____	_____	$ _____	$ _____

Subtotal $ _____

Deduct 10% when ordering 3-5 books $ _____

7.25% Sales Tax (CA only) $ _____

8.25% Sales Tax (TN only) $ _____

5.0% Sales Tax (MD and IN only) $ _____

Shipping and Handling* $ _____

Total Order $ _____

Shipping and Handling depend on Subtotal.

Subtotal	Shipping/Handling
$0.00–$14.99	$3.00
$15.00–$29.99	$4.00
$30.00–$49.99	$6.00
$50.00–$99.99	$10.00
$100.00–$199.99	$13.50
$200.00+	Call for Quote

Foreign and all Priority Request orders:
Call Order Entry department
for price quote at 916/632-4400

This chart represents the total retail price of books only
(before applicable discounts are taken).

By Telephone: With MC or Visa, call 800-632-8676, 916-632-4400. Mon-Fri, 8:30-4:30.
WWW {http://www.primapublishing.com}

Orders Placed Via Internet E-mail {sales@primapub.com}

By Mail: Just fill out the information below and send with your remittance to:

Prima Publishing
P.O. Box 1260BK
Rocklin, CA 95677

My name is _____

I live at _____

City_____ State_____ Zip _____

MC/Visa#_____ Exp._____

Check/Money Order enclosed for $_____ Payable to Prima Publishing

Daytime Telephone _____

Signature _____